Taking the Drudgery
Out of
Sermon Preparation

Taking the Drudgery
Out of
Sermon Preparation

Webb B. Garrison

BAKER BOOK HOUSE
Grand Rapids, Michigan

Formerly published under the title,
Creative Imagination in Preaching

ⓒ1960 by Abingdon Press
Paperback edition issued 1975
by Baker Book House Company
with permission of the copyright owner
ISBN: 0-8010-3698-4
Library of Congress
Catalog Card Number: 60-9197

To
Carol, Webb, and Bill

PREFACE

Most books for preachers devote a great deal of space to discussion of ways to arrange material into sermons. Comparatively little attention has been paid to the prior question of how to find ideas and illustrations. No degree of skill in preparing attention-catching introductions and well-balanced outlines quite provides the initial step in sermon preparation: having something fresh to say. Therefore, the focus of most chapters in the present study is upon the sublime and mysterious process of creativity.

Precisely how any one of us succeeds in getting an original idea, I do not know. It is beyond my capacity to suggest just where "discovery" ceases and "revelation" begins. Of this much, however, I am very certain: dialogue between God and man can proceed in many ways through a great variety of media. Skill in listening and observing can be cultivated in such fashion that everyday incidents lead to personal enlargement.

Because many such skills are analyzed, this study of the prelude to sermon writing falls in the category of the "how to do it" book. At the same time, I hope it is much more than that. Though technical terms are largely avoided, there is throughout a systematic attempt to present a philosophy of originality. Techniques and methods that are discussed can be considered in their own right. But only those who wholeheartedly believe that God can and does speak to all who give ear will receive maximum help from what is essentially an interpretation of creative listening.

This volume has taken its final form aided by the reactions and suggestions of many men. During the last decade, it has been my privilege to lecture in numerous one-week summer schools for pastors. Though many of the illustrative examples are new, all of the basic ideas here have been put to test in these schools. Original versions of most chapters have been modified as a result of questions and objections from preachers who heard them in lecture form.

Most of the stories and illustrations that are included come from my own experience. But for the sake of variety, and to foster adaptation by other users, many are described in the third person. Since the bulk of this volume consists of such material, it is a book of illustrations as well as an analysis of the way such stories are found.

There is one important concession to personal taste. Scripture quotations are from the King James Version. Although the Revised Standard Version and several vivid private translations are probably more suitable for young readers, the Authorized Version has a halo all its own. Since this quality contributed heavily to scriptural insights that bear on this book, it is natural to attempt to preserve that halo even in the fragmentary form of brief allusions.

My wife must have a special tribute here. She has been a daily source of comfort and challenge for nearly a quarter of a century. Moreover, she has been patient (usually) with my inattentiveness when I am squirming under the impact of an idea. And if she has been less than enthusiastic about encouraging it, she has tolerated my practice of pulling out cards and jotting down notes on all occasions.

I sincerely hope you will find pleasure as well as profit from striving to sharpen your own awareness of those divine messages that are everywhere about us.

—WEBB B. GARRISON

CONTENTS

1

How to Take the Drudgery Out of
Sermon Preparation

HOW MUCH TIME DO YOU SPEND PREPARING A SERMON? TOO
MUCH, you say immediately. You'll find much specific help
in this book, for the point of view and the methods presented
will cut the time spent in preparing to write sermons by fifty
to ninety per cent.

Perhaps you do not think of yourself as a professional writer.
But you certainly are. If you prepare only one new sermon each
week, you are producing at least 150,000 words a year. That is
more than the average output of the full-time writer whose entire time is devoted to his craft.

Your role as a witness to God requires you to write sermons
and talks in great volume during your whole career. But the
pressures of the modern church are so great that as God's spokes-
man you can give only a small portion of your time to this activity. You are required to be administrator, public relations direc-
tor, fund raiser, private counselor, and personnel chief.

Since you cannot give great blocks of undisturbed time to
preparation of sermons, the problem must be approached from
a new direction. One solution—perhaps the best that can be de-
vised—is that of stretching your time by using some of it differ-

13

ently. Many ways of doing this are suggested in subsequent chapters.

That Essential First Step

Most books on preaching center on how to organize and present material once it has been found. This book is different in that it has nothing to say on such matters. Instead, it comes to focus on the essential first step: finding ideas and insights. Compared with the matter of discovering new material, the task of arranging it into an orderly body of words is simple.

Some years ago, staff members of a national agency of an American church were asked to study the matter of style in writing and speaking. Each person in the group was like a parish minister in that he or she was continually engaged in communication. So it seemed desirable to sharpen skills a bit.

A visiting consultant was engaged for a special staff conference. He began his work by distributing a leaflet entitled "Fifteen Ways to Get People to Read What You Write." It analyzed in some detail such matters as length of words and sentences, use of short paragraphs, and the like.

One member of the group checked the entire list, then began to chuckle. For nowhere among the fifteen rules was one that advised the would-be writer or speaker, "First, have something to say."

It is easier to recognize the importance of having fresh ideas than to devise formulas to produce them. Partly because this is the case, our century has seen growing attention given to the matter of originality and creativity. Several general studies, attempting to suggest some factors that are involved in the mysterious process of thinking new thoughts, have been published.

Major strides have been taken. Artists, poets, scientists, musicians, and writers can now turn to a number of books which analyze both theories and practices that relate to this fascinating area of man's enlargement. Typical of such studies are *How to Think Creatively* by Eliot Dale Hutchinson[1] and *Creative Intuition in Art and Poetry* by Jacques Maritain.[2]

Even big business has been affected. Numerous books have been published for the benefit of advertising executives and copy writers, corporation presidents and assembly-line designers. *Applied Imagination* by Alex F. Osborn went through seven printings in three years.

If the process of getting ideas is significant to board chairmen as well as to poets, how much more crucial it is for preachers! Yet very little has been published in an attempt to apply the broad findings in this field to the work of spokesmen for God.

Most of this book is intensely practical. It suggests specific ways to increase the rate at which you discover fresh material for preaching. But this is not the only benefit promised. Two by-products of such activity are easing of work pressures and the joy of creative discovery.

Planning Reduces Pressure

Methods described in subsequent chapters will bring a sharp reduction in the effort required for your sermon writing. They are not so much concerned with "saving" time, however, as with making more fruitful use of it. Emphasis is placed upon ways to do the bulk of your preparation for preaching in time that is now barren.

One of the most famous essays of modern times is entitled "How to Live on 24 Hours a Day." Its chief emphasis is upon using small segments of time in constructive fashion. Nearly all of us waste brief periods every day. Over the years such short intervals attain importance.

Several well-worn stories are based upon this matter. According to one tale, a Norwegian merchant devoted his eightieth birthday to computing his use of time. He was surprised to find he had spent nearly five years waiting for people, three months scolding children, and six months tying neckties. Eight days were spent in telling dogs to lie down and be quiet!

Such a tale isn't meant to be taken seriously, but it has suggestive value. It emphasizes the fact that ten minutes one day and five the next, over a period of months or years, can be of importance. That is why better use of time that is being wasted or frittered away is a key to reducing pressures.

A day is like a suitcase. You can pack at least one-third more into it if you go about the task with care. Some persons just pile gear into the middle. But veteran travelers begin at the corners and sides. After packing them tightly, they fill in the middle.

More than most men, we preachers are subject to interruptions. We seldom have long periods in which to work on sermons. But we can pack our days like suitcases; for they hold much more when all the corners are filled.

In practice this can be done by adopting the habit of listening for God's voice in situations far removed from formal religious emphases. Instead of yielding to the incessant bombardment of secular noises, you can cultivate a mood of keeping one ear cocked for divine whispers. Such focus might be called "listening with the inner ear." In this book, awareness is the chief term used to name such striving to meet God.

Joy from Discovery

According to an African proverb, "Work only tires a woman—but it ruins a man!" In our fast-moving culture, it has become customary to regard work through even more jaundiced eyes. Work is regarded as a necessary evil, a burden to be carried because it cannot be avoided. It is a source of many vexations; large numbers of persons work chiefly in order to be able to afford the luxury of expensive hobbies and sports.

It follows that one way to reduce the work in a given set of activities is to find new joy through them. Pleasure transforms the context, changes a pattern of labor into a kind of recreation.

Most of our games, sports, and leisure-time activities yield fun through striving, overcoming, and mastering. These very elements figure largely in all creative tasks. It is no wonder that the unanimous witness of originators stresses the element of joy that stems from finding a new idea, solving a problem, or producing a work of art.

Jacques Maritain speaks of "the joy peculiar to the act of knowing." [3] He suggests that no pleasure quite matches that of thinking a new thought. Spinoza went so far as to identify pleasure generally with increase in understanding.

For us in the ministry, one of the most sublime sources of pleasure is that of hearing a message from God. It brings much more than the satisfaction of having something to say next Sunday. Along with insight into fresh truth, or a new aspect of old truth, there is likely to come joy that approaches ecstasy.

This is so familiar a component of religious experience that it is not necessary to multiply examples. But it is just as marked a factor in other situations involving enlargement—occasions in

17

which the creature made in the image of God succeeds briefly in playing the role of co-creator.

After solving a difficult problem, Sir Isaac Newton was often filled with such ecstasy that he had to stop work for a time. Revelations that led to discovery of analytic geometry left Descartes in a state of "radiant enthusiasm." Spinoza's intuitions, which led to many of his philosophical views, were accompanied by feeling so intense he could describe it only as "a sense of glory."

Perhaps the pleasure that accompanies insight stems from man's recognition that thinking a new thought is his most sublime achievement. If scientists and philosophers glory in discovery, how much more pleasure may a preacher derive from finding signs that point to God! When such creative moments abound, the finding of preaching material ceases to be "work."

2
Special Values of
Original Stories

SOME SERMONS ARE PUBLISHED IN BOOKS. MANY MORE ARE DIS-
tributed in the form of leaflets and as digests in parish papers.
But in its broad application to life, the sermon is a special vehicle
for oral, rather than written, communication.

In some respects, the spoken word has advantages over the
same message in print. For when reduced to a pattern of black
marks on white paper, a sermon loses the vitality that comes from
gestures, emphasis, and tone of voice. Shades of meaning are
more likely to be lost in writing than in speaking.

Moreover, the man who stands before a congregation and
speaks directly to its members has some guarantee that he will
be heard. Though levels of attention vary widely, each person
in an audience is encouraged by the situation to listen. That
is not the case with written material; the reader is subject to
many more distractions than the listener. He is likely to be
interrupted repeatedly by the radio, television, telephone, door-
bell, members of the family, and visitors.

Yet it is a mistake to conclude that special features of face-to-
face communication through spoken words make this situation
easy. For there are disadvantages in oral communication as compared with written.

When a reader comes to a sentence or paragraph that puzzles him, he may ponder its meaning. If necessary, he turns back and re-reads. He is not required to snatch little clusters of meaning on the wing, as it were. For him, the "one chance only" quality of understanding a word or phrase from the pulpit is absent.

Again, when ideas and challenges are put into print, the writer may point the reader to sources of quotations and to additional helps. At best, such devices are awkward in a sermon delivered from the pulpit. Footnotes tend to clutter up oral communication, and frequently do more harm than good.

This brief survey does not begin to exhaust the matter. It does, however, indicate that the preacher must function in a highly specialized type of communication. Lacking many advantages that attach to the written word, he must speak with vigor and authority in order to hold attention and persuade men.

Because of this aspect of our task, firsthand stories and interpretations are especially significant. Many that lack sufficient "body" for use in print are effective from the pulpit. To the degree that you can use your own vivid experiences and discoveries as raw material for sermons, you overcome many disadvantages of the spoken word as compared with the written.

Freshness Compels Attention

As the last of his passengers scrambled for seats, the driver of a bus rapped for attention. He welcomed us aboard, then called the route:

"Folks, this is your bus for Jacksonville, Atlanta, Charlotte, Asheville, Knoxville, Cookeville, and Lebanon, Tennessee."

Instead of screening out his words as we usually do with a routine announcement, I gave that driver my entire attention.

Five minutes earlier, the dispatcher had told me that the Knox-ville bus would leave from position number one; this was the right place and time. My destination was called by the driver —but there was something startlingly different about his an-nouncement.

Reflection quickly revealed that the driver had called cities of his route in reverse order. His list began at the terminus and worked back to the city of origin. When questioned, he grinned. "Since I started doing it this way, I've never had a passenger on the wrong bus," he said. "This way, everybody sits up and takes notice before we get out on the highway."

Because we have heard the route announced many times, we do not always listen when cities on life's highway are enumerated in church. Even a slight change in the pattern will prod many travelers into giving full attention. Virtually ignored in the familiar old version, any message will receive a hearing when given a fresh twist.

The requirement of freshness is particularly significant in situations where a preacher seeks for twenty minutes to hold the attention of listeners who vary widely in age, personal in-terests, educational background, and commitment to the Chris-tian goal. But the pulpit is not alone in its demand for vital new material. Writing on *The Aims of Education*—and all com-munication is a kind of education—Alfred North Whitehead insists that

For successful education there must always be a certain freshness in the knowledge dealt with. It must either be new in itself or it must be invested with some novelty of application to the new world of new times. Knowledge does not keep any better than fish.[1]

When we have found fresh messages uniquely our own and dynamic because they come from experience, our sentences will cease to be rhetorical arrangements of words. Rather, they will become "arrows from the bow of imagination, barbed, feathered, aimed, quivering—made for the target."

Give this quality of freshness whatever label you wish—listener interest, entertainment value, novelty appeal—it is something every member of an audience is seeking all the time, whether consciously or not. Coleridge describes his Ancient Mariner as having so vivid a tale to tell that he held his listeners with his glittering eye. It is only the rarely gifted evangelist who can in some degree succeed in holding a congregation with his glittering eye.

Most of us have to rely on words. Our sermons need what might be called "lapel quality"—intangible freshness that will hold a man by the lapel of his coat while late word from the Lord is poured into his ears.

From Life to Life

Even if it should be fresh and never before heard, material that is a product of other minds and situations must be used with caution. Too great a dependence upon it tends to create a gulf between the pulpit and life. Even the great thoughts of the immortals are seldom wholly effective when used verbatim.

Unless one has lived with secondhand material until it undergoes subtle transformations and becomes literally his own, it is likely to be somewhat abstract and theoretical—academic. Like the counterfeit coin that can be detected only by its sound, a borrowed message may look perfect but seldom ring true.

One of the bases for this phenomenon, hard to reduce to a

22

formula but easy to recognize in practice, is the effect of the audience upon a message. Though identical words may be used, no sermon is ever preached twice in identical fashion. Those who listen to it have profound effects upon the way it is heard.

It follows that a message is affected by its audience, which is the target for words of a writer or speaker. Much material that was dynamic when written fails to make contact with persons whose interests are different. That is why it is hard to make good use of anecdotes from the funeral of Lord Shaftesbury, Voltaire's attacks on the Bible, G. Campbell Morgan's encounters with skeptics, and the like.

Effective preaching material must be discovered, selected, and adapted to communicate with those who make up a specific audience. Classical and academic allusions, readily utilized by the reader, are not so readily received by the listener. Comparatively trivial experiences out of everyday life are more likely to make effective contact with listeners than are accounts of world-shaking events not linked with here and now.

One of the largest department stores in the world, the J. L. Hudson Company, employs a group of experts in its advertising department. These trained users of words find it difficult to retain the life-centered approach. So each copy writer has on his desk a little wooden figure representing "Mrs. Murphy." She is depicted as a typical housewife—and stands with arms akimbo to remind word users that communication means talking with her.

It is the role of the listener which accounts for the way a single down-to-earth incident can persuade more effectively than much exhortation. While this matter is central in preaching, it is not limited to this form of communication.

Some years ago, a legislator set out to get an appropriation to extend services of public health agencies. In spite of brochures of statistics and reports by doctors, it was apparent that the bill would not pass. Two hours before the vote was to be taken, its sponsor distributed a three-by-five card to each member of the legislature. It included no technical data, no testimony from experts. Instead, it told this story:

A widowed mother of three small children received a routine chest x-ray and was told she had tuberculosis. She could not get treatment without giving up her job—and if she did that, her children would be without support. She requested help from state health agencies, but was told they had no funds. So Mrs. Robinson went home to die —determined to care for Robert and Norman and Sarah as long as she could lift her tired hands.

That same day, a farmer in her county noticed signs of cholera in his brood sow. He sent a telegram to a state official. Next day, a veterinarian made a trip to his farm, gave the hog treatment and cured it.

Moral: Be a hog!

Inevitably, the health bill passed. Lawmakers were challenged by an emotion-charged incident from life close at hand. So they responded in a fashion quite different from that evoked by secondhand arguments and academic evidence. Listeners to sermons react in the same way.

A Voice of Authority

As a young preacher in rural South Carolina, I sometimes led evangelistic services. One evening before the first service of a series, I had supper with the family of the Sunday-school superintendent. He introduced me to his wife and children as "the visiting preacher."

24

One of the boys, who must have been four or five years old, stared at me intently. Finally he blurted, "You're not a preacher!"

Probing to discover the basis of that verdict, his mother extracted an explanation, "Mamma, he can't be a preacher. He's got too much hair!"

Never having seen a minister other than his own bald pastor, the child had established hair—or, rather, the lack of it—as the criterion by which to identify preachers.

After all, one might ask, what *is* the unique factor by which an evangelical minister is distinguished?

It is not in his right to perform the marriage ceremony, for that may be done by justices of the peace. It does not lie in his duty to bury the dead, for the captain of a ship officiates at sea. It is not in his giving of the sacraments, for some churches have none. It is not derived from his skill in looking after business of a local church; laymen can do a better job.

One thing—and one only—sets the preacher apart from the rest of men: he is assumed to speak with authority on matters of the spirit. Such authority on the part of a leader conveys a subtle but real sense of certainty to his followers. Accepting the leadership of Joshua, the Israelites had but one plea: "Only be strong and of a good courage" (Josh. 1:18).

Without a vital sense of assurance in the pulpit, which passes from thence to the pew, no number of "programs" can keep the roof from sagging. "No serious treatment of religion dare be over-modest," warns Hocking.[2]

Among syndicated comic strips, one of the few that remains humorous is entitled "Pogo." Its name is derived from that of a delightful little creature who lives in the great Okefeenokee Swamp.

Some time ago Pogo was sitting with his back propped against a fallen log. A strange animal came along the trail and Pogo stopped him. He demanded that the intruder give his name and tell what kind of animal he might be. Politely enough, the newcomer explained that he was a carrier pigeon.

Pogo was unacquainted with the species, so he asked his new acquaintance what he carried. That was easy, the pigeon explained. He carried messages.

Still skeptical, Pogo insisted on proof. Nothing would satisfy him but seeing a message. Confronted by this demand, the pigeon hung his head. "I had a message," he explained. "But I put it in my shoe. Done walked so long I wore a hole in the sole, an' lost my message through the hole."

A messenger without a message! That is the dilemma of the preacher who cannot speak with authority, having nothing vital to offer from his own experience. One cannot persuade others to accept his goals and loyalties until he vigorously makes them public.

An executive of a major advertising firm insists that an intangible sense of authority is necessary in selling goods as well as spreading faith. "I think it would be very productive to scout college campuses for those boys who not only like to write," he says, "but who are messianic in life, who want to convert people to their point of view—because this is the basis of advertising." [3]

Plato's famous *Symposium* includes the testimony of a scholar who said:

When I listen to Pericles or any other orator of the day, I say to myself, "He is a good speaker," and that is all; but when I listen to

Socrates, my soul is stirred, my eyes fill with tears, and I blush for the trivialities on which I spend my days.[4]

Though such authority in preaching grows out of much more than the use of life-centered stories, materials of this sort are far more potent than most secondhand ones. Stories and examples that come from your own experience are not only fresh and life-centered; attached to them is the dynamic that comes from the joy of discovery. Consequently, your original material can be shared with others more effectively than that which is borrowed unchanged from any preacher or writer, however vigorous.

3

All Things Are Soaked with Potential for Revelation

ALL THINGS SPEAK TO THOSE WHO LISTEN WITH EARS RIGHTLY attuned.

That is the primary message of this book; but in order to discover its dynamic, you must accept some views that are beyond the kinds of proof demanded in academic disciplines. These propositions can be put to use only through living faith.

By even skeptical use of some practices indicated in succeeding chapters, you can increase your skill in finding ideas and illustrations. But in order to stumble upon deep truths, to come into life-shaking personal encounter with God through everyday events, it is essential that you give allegiance to these assumptions:

1. Profound meaning permeates every area of experience. The concept "meaningless" must be rejected. All events are soaked with potential for revelation.

2. Signs that point to God are prepared for the receptive eye. Viewed by the natural man, they do not reveal their deepest truths: "they are foolishness unto him: neither can he know them, because they are spiritually discerned" (I Cor. 2:14).

There is no limit to the number and type of God's revealing works. Some men see none; others find the category exhausted

28

in nature's more spectacular glories. Still others find God in the commonplace.

Each of us is a ceaselessly-active organizing center. All that we encounter is either placed in the card catalogue of our understanding, or rejected as meaningless. But meaning is not a quality that attaches to raw items of experience. Rather, it is a fruit of the relationship between person and event. All events are rich in potential for revelation, but only those who succeed in establishing relationships will discover meanings.

Coherence Required

An Illinois truckers' stop advertises fine food by using highway signs to lure customers. Its crumb-littered counters contrast sharply with the neat billboards proclaiming the merits of the place.

A traveler stopped for coffee a few months ago, and noticed a hand-lettered placard above the glass rack. Fastened to the wall with cellophane tape, it proclaimed: "WE RESERVE THE RIGHT TO SEAT OUR CUSTOMERS." After absorbing the message, the visitor glanced about the room. There were plenty of stools. No one seemed to have a problem about being seated.

Reflection suggests two possible interpretations. This restaurant may be operated by an officer of the W.C.T.U. who wants the right to refuse service to a drunk. Or the polite notice may be a legal way of preserving racial segregation in the land of Lincoln.

No matter which alternative you support, you will reach your decision by the coherence test. In the light of all your understanding, one set of ideas about that seating policy "fits." So a never-before encountered sign can be placed in ordered relationship with prior experiences. When you have put the new event in its place, like a piece fitted into a jigsaw puzzle, you suddenly say: "Yes, I understand!" That is, by placing the event within a relationship, it has acquired meaning.

Our God-given minds, beside which electronic calculating machines are crude toys, operate so swiftly and effectively that we seldom observe their workings. It is only in strange situations that we gain the perspective to notice activities we take for granted.

On a Sunday in July, my wife and I sat in the big auditorium at Lake Junaluska, N. C. Because the boys were restless, we were seated far to one side—separated from other worshipers by thirty feet. A hymn was announced and 1,500 voices were lifted in Frances R. Havergal's petition, "Lord, speak to me."

Our isolation forced recognition that sung words are different from spoken ones. In much vocal music, words are subordinate to tone patterns. Syllable division and stress in sung words make them hardly intelligible to one familiar only with spoken versions of the same words.

Near incoherence would result from a solemn congregational prayer in which the speaker intoned: "Lord, spe-eak to me-e, that I-I may speak." Yet within a familiar context you and I take this pattern in stride without so much as noticing it. Through experience we have formed systems into which split-syllable words of hymns fit neatly.

Yet the structure of experience that you take for granted may give me trouble. No two of us live in identical worlds. Even persons with similar cultural backgrounds may react quite differently to a given signal.

30

Charles A. Bennett says he once sat musing in a train. His eye was caught by a billboard. So he looked up, startled, to read: "Gorton's God, no bones." [1] Had he been a sportsman or chef rather than a theologian, stimuli forming the word "Cod" would never have been seen as a pointer toward God. His experience and interests affected the way his mind organized visual cues. Whatever one's orientation, the same process operates.

Perhaps H. G. Wells expressed the matter for all time. Writing on "Scepticism of the Instrument," he suggested that forceps of the mind are clumsy, and crush truth a bit in grasping it.

Yet grasp it, they do. So the seeker who aims at understanding some of God's invisible things by the light of the visible discovers clues everywhere he turns. Any event has the capacity to shed light when brought into relationship with a questioning and believing soul.

No meaning lies in an event that has not been met, or in a mind that shuts out encounter by entering a state such as madness or complacency. Barring such a situation, failure to find messages in everyday experience is due to indifference or skepticism or dullness of eyes and ears.

This idea is central to the biblical outlook. According to it God is involved in all that can be met. Any event seen through the eyes of expectant belief will take its place in an ordered system of experiences and yield its special message.

Bending by the Mind

Departing from the cowboy theme, a television drama centered about a small-town sheriff's treatment of his prisoner. Arrested for having violated the speed limit by five miles per hour, a traveler was unable to pay his fine. Jailed because he

31

argued the case, he was grilled by the officer—up for re-election —who jumped to the conclusion that the prisoner was a hit-and-run killer.

One TV analyst used his whole battery of adjectives to criticize that play. As a story, he said, it was too thin a vehicle for the talented actors who were involved.

My wife and I strongly objected to his analysis. Both of us sat spellbound, chewing our nails, throughout the drama. She had recently been arrested and fined in an Illinois village whose justice of the peace was barely literate. I had been captured and bullied late at night in Indiana, far from home.

Experience is the key. The critic would not have felt the story drab had he ever been signaled to a halt at 1:30 A.M. with no friend within a hundred miles, and forced at gunpoint to give his driver's license to a hulking trooper whose authority was absolute and who had become a little Hitler under the cancerous effects of conscious power.

Always the observing mind bends objects and events. That anguished soul, William Blake, gave vivid expression to the universal witness of poets and artists when he insisted that "everybody does not see alike."

Seen through eyes of a miser, he suggested, a gold piece is literally more beautiful than the sun. A worn moneybag has lovelier lines than a grape-filled vine. "The tree which moves some to tears of joy is in the Eyes of others only a Green thing which stands in the way," he said.[2]

Twenty-five centuries ago the philosopher Heraclitus put it like this: "Eyes and ears are bad witnesses to those who have barbarian souls." [3] Richness or poverty of my experience affects my capacity to find meaning in a given event. What I see is a fruit of my personal viewing.

A central figure in the play *Romanoff and Juliet* is a dictator in a tiny principality. After a life of military service, he sees everything through the eyes of a soldier. So he addresses the dawn as "the hour of the last glass of brandy," "the hour of the firing squad." Such meanings would not occur to a poet whose attitude toward sunrise is based on familiarity with lyric verse.

As with traffic officers, trees, and the rising of the sun, so with all encounters between minds and things. Bending by the mind is basic and cannot be eliminated. That is the key to the scriptural motif which warns that the natural man has eyes but does not see, has ears but does not hear.

Pharisees sneered at naïve ideas of the man whose blindness was healed by washing in the pool of Siloam. To veteran interpreters of the law it was ridiculous that one "altogether born in sins" should suggest new meanings to them. In repudiating his discoveries these experts supported a still popular view of learning. According to it all knowledge can be wrapped in neat bundles and transmitted without loss from one person to another.

Such a view minimized the dynamic role of the learner. Given special receptivity, an eager amateur can make discoveries from material that communicates nothing new to those respected as erudite.

A major accusation by Amos against his contemporaries centered in this matter. For to the shepherd-prophet, there were vital God-linked meanings in such matters as the roar of a lion, the sight of a mangled sheep, the coming of grasshoppers, and a basket of fruit.

Amos and a host of other sensitive men witness that only a God-centered mind so bends raw materials of experience that all things convey divine messages.

Molding by the Culture

Among the most distinctive movies of recent years is a Japanese production entitled *Samurai*. Filmed in Japan, it employed oriental writers, actors, and technicians. Color photography is superbly imaginative; the use of blues in some scenes stirs moods as effectively as Whistler's one-tone paintings.

An ancient legend is the basis of the action. Laid in feudal Japan, it centers in a period of civil war. Great men of the era who gave their lives to the task of unifying the land were honored as Samurai.

A village peasant, hero of the movie, has great animal courage but little finesse. He proves his mettle by defeating a band of outlaws. Captured, he is thrown in contact with an orphan girl —who frees him and flees with him. Recaptured, he is given the task of studying in order to gain wisdom.

After three years he is made Samurai and offered a post of honor. He refuses it in order to travel in search of greater wisdom. His sweetheart, whom he loves tenderly and has had in his thoughts daily, comes to him in a joyful reunion. Before its glow has faded, he sends her to pack in order to go with him on his search for maturity. She returns to the rendezvous to find him gone, having scratched on the rail of the bridge the plea: "Forgive me." On that note, the story ends.

Every viewer is entitled to ask whether or not it comes out right.

Answers will depend upon one's values and goals. To Americans who are dominated by Hollywood's views of love, *Samurai* certainly does not come out right. But from the viewpoint of sixteenth-century Japanese, the story would have been all wrong had it ended in a fashion other than desertion of his sweetheart by a Samurai who placed service above self.

It is common knowledge that works of literature and music and art are variously received by persons of various periods. Sören Kierkegaard was all but unintelligible to most nineteenth-century Danes. But in today's tortured civilization his fevered pleas stir multitudes. Vincent van Gogh had difficulty in giving away his paintings during his life; now they are fought over by wealthy collectors who view them from a different cultural perspective.

Dante's *Divine Comedy* rocked fourteenth-century Europe— but is far from a best seller today. *Pilgrim's Progress* and *Gulliver's Travels* have met the same fate. But William Blake, who had no contemporary audience, is now widely read.

How are we to account for so marked a pattern of change in opinion?

Influence of critics aside, a painting or book or musical composition has different effects on persons with different backgrounds. Not only does individual experience bend the meaning found in an event; social forces also exert molding effects.

In some periods, people have been peculiarly sensitive to spiritual things. Cultural orientation has been in the direction of encouraging men to listen for divine messages in the slightest whispers. Conspicuous examples are ancient Israel intoxicated by Jehovah and medieval Europe enamored with Christ.

Upon encounter with the new and out of the ordinary, men may react in a variety of ways. That which is beyond easy ex-

35

planation may be linked with chance, demonic forces, or error. Or it may be referred to God.

This last approach is that of Scripture. Any event that may be encountered is assumed to fit within the context of providence. This conclusion is reached in faith; but until it is accepted, we are limited in our capacity to search for divine messages.

By and large, the pervasive influence of today's culture tends to reduce our tendency to see a Creator at work in all events. So in addition to fostering our innate capacity to bend meanings God-ward, preachers must now strive to combat the molding power of pervasive secularism. That the task of achieving keen vision is difficult only makes its rewards more thrilling.

4
God's Messages Are Prepared for Receptive Eyes

POTENTIAL FOR REVELATION IS UNLIMITED. ALL THINGS THAT HAVE been made can foster understanding of their Maker. Nothing is without power to convey a message from God to a prepared mind.

That is the thesis of Calvin's introductory comments with which he began his *Institutes*. Man is equipped with a "sensus divinitatis," he said. By use of it, anyone can find innumerable evidences of the Creator.

Discoveries do not come in automatic fashion, though. The capacity to establish a particular pattern of understanding is affected by both individual and cultural factors. Profound discoveries about God and life are most likely to be made by those who seek them in vital belief. That is, all the world has been made ready to participate in pointing us to God—but has been prepared especially for those with receptive eyes.

Fostered by Tradition

Attitude makes some situations more likely than others to evoke religious moods and discoveries. When we enter a place of public worship, our eyes are naturally focused on things of God. This factor makes a prayer chapel or other place of private worship a likely setting for discovery.

Cultural endorsement also makes the more sublime aspects of nature function as pointers to God. Men of modern America concur with those of ancient Israel in saying that Jehovah is praised by voices of mountains, hills, and cedars, as well as by sun, moon, and stars. It takes no special sensitivity to feel awe when standing at the peak of Clingman's Dome or peering at Mars through a telescope.

Sacred art and music help create and sustain awareness of signals. From a solemn concert of Brahms' works to the booming of a hymn by Tennessee Ernie Ford, "religious" cues are likely to stimulate consciousness of God. Part of this effect is due to the material employed by the painter or musician. Part of it stems from the fact that the universe is viewed through spectacles of faith when our attention is directed toward God.

Other sets of stimuli have come to be regarded as religiously oriented through influence of sensitive interpreters. Tennyson once plucked a flower from the niche where it fought for life. As he held it, the poet felt an overwhelming sense of life's grandeur. He and other writers expressed this discovery vividly, and so magnified the tendency to see God in a flower.

Certain situations and contexts have become religiously charged. It is common to find them suggesting new discoveries. That being the case, it seems logical that conscious seeking for messages from God in all things will make "secular" situations as fruitful as "sacred."

Such is precisely the case.

Magnified by Interest

Dominant interests, whether momentary or life-directed, help to focus attention and enhance discovery. Just as the mood of an occasion affects all who are caught up in it, so the outlook of an individual gives tone to all of his situations.

Eagerly anticipating his twelfth Christmas, one boy came to focus his yearnings in a nifty pair of track shoes. He vowed he wanted nothing else—and would take no substitute. Riding to town for a family shopping expedition, nearly everything shouted: "Track shoes!"

For example, his aunt commented that trade was slack where she worked, but that they had nice leather goods. "Track shoes are made of leather," the boy said. During his obsession, any word or object remotely linked with his Christmas hopes had power to evoke shoe-centered meanings.

Plautus described a woman so eager for clues to her dominant interest that she went about the Roman world "playing the hunter with her eyes and bird-watcher with her ears." Such a state of receptivity, oriented toward Jehovah, marked the psalmists of Israel. Psalm 1 comes from meditation so directed that deep meanings are found in a tree growing by a river, a fresh unwithered leaf, a cluster of ripe fruit, and a farmer tossing his grain.

An appetite for such spiritual delicacies can be cultivated. One who never ate ripe olives or anchovies or Roquefort cheese in childhood can establish fondness for these dainties by nibbling them. Just so, conscious enjoyment of signs from God will foster yearning for more. Thomas S. Kepler says he seldom comes to a street intersection without thinking of the Cross. Because he is cross-conscious, intersecting boulevards take him to Calvary.

Lowell devotes one of his most powerful poems to discounting the notion that God spoke more loudly in the time of Moses

39

than now. A wilderness wanderer who sees no clue of Sinai is a victim of his own blindness, suggests the poet. For the mountain of the voice goes unnoticed by one who is absorbed with gathering manna. Conversely, anything can witness to one whose interest serves to magnify cues. Signs of God abound even in the slums of Tokyo—if one has the eyes of a Kagawa.

To the eager listener, "The voice of the Lord breaketh the cedars" (Ps. 29:5). Recognition of this wonder involves more than a beautiful metaphor. For since the human voice produces minute vibrations in air, it is not a strained analogy to make storm blasts an effect of divine speaking.

So regarded, what do the winds say? As with air waves of human origin, there is only noise and babble to listeners ignorant of the language. But a sensitive interpreter hears the howling of the storm and crashing of great cedars and finds in those sounds the mesage that Jehovah rules.

Carefully scrutinizing the horizon after a summer shower, the skeptic vows that he nowhere finds a trace of God. The ardent believer views a rainbow and finds the bent bow of the Lord of Hosts—"a token of the covenant between me and the earth" (Gen. 9:13).

Camouflaged by Convention

No matter how suggestive an event may be, an observer who has a well-established set of understandings will find it hard to see anything new. For the power of the familiar is such that even a few repetitions of a pattern may camouflage all meanings except the one already recognized.

In a day of abundant highways and bridges, few pause to marvel at the ease with which a watercourse may be crossed.

We have lost the viewpoint of Israel's herdsmen, who glorified Jehovah at the wonder of his providence by which men could sometimes cross a river dry-shod. Our contemporary way of taking bridges for granted stems from our failure to look at them with eyes of faith. For those who are eager to see the Creator at work, the simplest river crossing shouts of God's marvels.

Jesus looked at commonplace things in such fashion that the veneer of convention disappeared. So many of his messages are startlingly bold. But in order to see them as challenging, the layers of familiarity in which they are swathed must be removed.

We tend to be casual in accepting as a commonplace the idea that whoever does the will of God becomes "my brother, and my sister, and mother" (Mark 3:35). Actually, this daring metaphor is soaked with emotional overtones. To give a fresh twist to a word or idea is to create a verbal spotlight that reveals dazzling new truth until it, too, becomes so much a part of the cultural inheritance that men use it from childhood and look through it rather than at it.

Surrounded since infancy by the astonishing gifts of God, our eyes are covered with film so that we usually fail to see how brilliantly the gems of nature do glitter. Francis of Assisi succeeded in washing some of the film from his eyes. Hence he viewed ordinary things as unexpected fruits of divine bounty. So regarded, the rising of the sun became a birthday present, and the shade of a poplar a marvelous gift fashioned with painstaking care by a Father who counts nothing too good for his children.

The Pharisees witnessed many miracles, but saw no signs pointing to God. There is but one explanation: they were blind to much evidence. Their very skill in debating technical issues within the accepted system was a handicap to them in seeing fresh truth. For them neither the sign of Jonas nor the empty tomb conveyed the message that Christ is Lord of Life. When their eardrums rattled from the booming of a heavenly voice, they said it was thunder.

One of the reasons for blindness of the Pharisees was their loyalty to established interpretations. Inability to see new meanings constituted the "leaven of the Pharisees." Those whose lives are affected by such leaven can gather evidence to support the conclusions which they already accept. But it is difficult for them to find fresh truth in any experience that constitutes a message so new that its ink is still wet from the pen of God!

How many ancients sat for days on end in the potter's house and saw only a wheel, clay, and the nimble fingers of an artisan?

So long as familiar meanings dominate the mind, no fresh message can emerge. But when the camouflage of conventional understanding is pulled aside by a Jeremiah, the voice of the Lord will speak—even in the squeaking of a potter's wheel.

5
Every Man Can
See Visions

FLIGHT NUMBER THREE TO LOUISVILLE TOOK OFF PROMPTLY AT 10:46. As the plane climbed gradually in passing over Asheville, we caught a clear glimpse of the palatial Biltmore Estates. A small private lake came into view and faded under a bridge that revealed startlingly graceful lines.

Without quite knowing when it happened, I found that my attention had shifted from the ground to masses of clouds. At first they seemed to rush past at cabin level. Then two layers were clearly visible—one above us and one far below. Everywhere clouds dominated the visual field.

A cloud is a dynamic system of air and water, engaged in constant change. It has neither precise shape nor definite edges. No conceivable system of micromeasurements would establish its exact size and shape.

Yet the reality of a cloud is as great as that of a Bureau of Standards pound. A cumulus layer not susceptible to measurement may be seen and may be detected by radar. It casts a shadow, transports a burden, and is solidly felt when entered by a plane!

Clouds are just as real as bricks, but they cannot be so neatly defined or so precisely measured. Both bricks and clouds are objects of experience, but they differ in the degree to which they can be understood on the basis of evidence gathered with a foot rule.

Hosts of men eager to know both the created world and its Creator have insisted that spiritual truths differ from material truths as clouds differ from bricks. According to such a view, God's self-unfolding is both leading men and continually "making wise the simple" (Ps. 19:7).

Here is a neat paradox! A simple one who ponders the law of the Lord is not made wise. Rather, he is both simple and wise simultaneously. Mastery of knowledge is not the other side of the coin that is stamped wisdom of God. Wisdom and simplicity can coexist; they are not mutually exclusive.

Knowledge deals with "facts" which rest upon evidence gathered with our senses. It is knowledge that constitutes the domain of science. Knowledge permits us to order our lives so that we can survive on earth. Knowledge can be incorporated into a formula without significant loss of content.

Wisdom is different in kind from knowledge, and rests on non-sensory encounter with the seeking Spirit of God. Learning is not essential to wisdom; one can be quite ignorant and yet very wise in the ways of God. Man's quest for wisdom is the theme of the Old Testament: "Teach me thy statutes" is the yearning refrain of Israel's entire literary heritage.

Knowledge of material sort can be fully communicated through words and other symbols. It can be transmitted from one generation to another without major distortion. It can be learned by effort of the will.

Wisdom is mysterious, beyond logic, less than fully communi-

44

cable. To the end it must remain "the hidden wisdom" (I Cor. 2:7). Men do not gain it by philosophic, legal, or scientific study. It differs in nature—not merely in degree—from the knowledge of savants.

Yet it is not wholly elusive. In halting fashion, we can both examine the nature of the experience we seek and devise some ways to preserve and make public its fruits.

Radiant with Meaning

Invoking divine inspiration, Charles Wesley begins a famous hymn with the plea, "Come, Holy Ghost, our hearts inspire." Using a vivid metaphor from the psalms, he compares the shelter of Providence with protective wings of a mother fowl and urges:

> Expand Thy wings, celestial Dove,
> Brood o'er our nature's night;
> On our disordered spirits move,
> And let there now be light.

That is, the sensitive poet-preacher sought for himself and for us a special mood: a soul-state in which light comes from outside to reveal new things within. Though it may be more, such a mood is at least the moment of artistic "inspiration" with dominant religious qualities. It has much in common with the instant of creative "invention" by a Galileo or an Einstein, but is oriented toward God instead of the created order.

Attempts to express the nature of the visionary state are always stammering. Sometimes it comes as a fruit of seeking; frequently it descends uninvited and takes control, as it were. That is especially the case when emotional currents are strong.

Before he recognized his literary talent, Somerset Maugham

studied medicine. He graduated at London's St. Thomas Hospital, and in order to gain his certificate was required to serve a period of internship. During one period he was assigned to emergency wards, where he was on call for victims of accidents. Recalling this intimate relationship with life and death, he said such work left him "tired out but wonderfully exhilarated." [1]

Evelyn Underhill goes so far as to suggest that such reactions are typical because emotion affects the whole person and not simply the mind.

Not long after this matter was discussed with a group of ministers, two of them sent me supporting testimony from their own experience.

Dr. John Wesley Kennedy of West Virginia described his most memorable hours in a chaplain's uniform:

Late one night our colonel returned from division headquarters and had a meeting of his staff in the wobbling ruins of a farm building. He told us to keep it from the men, but to understand that we had been ordered to proceed until stopped . . . . We were expendable.

He turned to me and suggested that I'd better pray.

Next morning we moved up to the point of departure with orders to wait until daybreak for the zero hour. That early evening, beside my foxhole in the midst of the men, in an open tree-lined field, I was aware of a compassion and a benevolence I had never possessed. Peculiarly, I had a vast tenderness toward the grass, the tree line and the sky with its drifting evening clouds. I seemed to have a second sight, and quiet but exalted love for all creation.

Similar language was used by an army major who knelt at the altar to take vows of church membership and entered a mood experienced just once before, late in World War II.

Germans were throwing all the mortars and shells they had into the area where we had dug in. All hell broke loose, it seemed. The next day was Sunday. The Germans had retreated. The sunshine cast shadows into the crater a few feet from my foxhole. Everything was quiet—everything but a tiny bird sitting on a single strand of barbed wire and singing its heart out. Serenity and calm came upon me, and suddenly I saw God revealed through the song of the bird.

These examples do not exhaust the meaning of the creative mood, but they do indicate that fleeting moments of heightened awareness can come to all.

Subject to Cultivation

No seeker can hope to attain full control of the mood of inspiration. It comes and goes involuntarily. There are moments when it descends unheralded and takes command. At other seasons sensitivity vanishes in spite of the soul's yearning that it continue.

Capacity to scale heights during receptive moods is affected by both personality and total set of organized beliefs. It takes a rare combination of factors to make a potential Augustine or Meister Eckhart.

Yet all of us have some degree of innate capacity to receive divine signals, and that special capacity is subject to cultivation. We ordinary, nonmystical folk are fond of hymns in which we pray, "Open my eyes, that I may see" and rejoice, "I once was blind, but now I see!"

Much of the burden of this book comes to focus at this point. For by conscious cultivation of our God-given capacity to see flashes of divine light and to hear whispers from the Creator, all of us will be flooded with firsthand discoveries.

Humility is an essential ingredient in the compound that fosters illumination. "If any man among you seemeth to be wise in this world, let him become a fool, that he may be wise." (I Cor. 3:18.)

Wisdom, in the sense of recognized mastery of facts, serves as an inhibitor. Whether the subject matter be differential equations or the law of Moses is a matter of indifference.

Consciousness of limitedness is the first step toward gaining power. He who recognizes himself to be lost, blind, and impotent is ready to accept that wisdom which consists in being rather than knowing. This is quite a different matter from muttering clichés about one's humility.

It involves vital personal encounter with truth of the sort hinted at in the promise that "the Lord looseth the prisoners: The Lord openeth the eyes of the blind" (Ps. 146:7-8). Intellectually, you and I are prisoners of a socially transmitted set of factors essential to group life: words, thought forms, values, beliefs, loyalties, and ideas.

We cannot become human without accepting these things and learning to use them. But once acquired, each plays the role of the Old Man of the Sea, and becomes increasingly heavy as we stagger toward new experiences.

Part of the act of divine release consists in freeing us from the prisons of knowledge so we may explore the paths of understanding. Before I can walk through the unlocked door of my cell, I must recognize that I am imprisoned. In order to see, I must confess that I am blind.

Receptivity is even more difficult to describe and define than is intellectual humility; but it is equally vital to the visionary mood. Striving is a precondition. Man must seek—with all his power; but he must also be willing to sit quietly and wait for the tap of a divine messenger on his door. Too much frenzied striving will have him always out in the forest searching with a flashlight, so that he is away when a messenger comes to his door.

A degree of resignation and surrender is a factor in all secular as well as religious discovery, creativity, conversion, and sudden enlargement. Its role is somewhat like that of the invisible beam that controls a door with an electric eye. The door will not open until one has stepped to the right spot. But on reaching it, he does not have to push—the door opens without effort on the visitor's part.

Relaxed attention has the strange effect of fostering discovery of things overlooked in concentration. Charles Wesley testifies to this factor in his plea that the Spirit "brood o'er our nature's night."

In the sunlight of intense thought, everything is seen in customary outlines—as approved and acknowledged within the culture. When the moonlight of relaxation bathes the same scene, unsuspected contours and never-before discovered shapes emerge.

It is not accidental that the Psalmist witnesses to his conviction that he receives instruction "in the night seasons" (Ps. 16:7). Creative listening is fostered by the physical night, which encourages relaxation in lieu of the sharply focused attention of working hours.

The mental night which comes from shutting out claimants for attention is fully as revealing as the night that shuts out sunlight. When one concentrates upon sounds and shapes and colors that make up the everyday world, the soul's receiving set is so tuned that no extraordinary signals can be received. To discover

49

new things, we must look through eyes focused with a trifle less than conventional sharpness.

An example from low-level awareness will help to suggest what must be experienced in order to be understood.

While I was worshiping on a Sunday when the service dragged along interminably, my attention gradually shifted from speakers to the back of the pew immediately in front of me. A quite ordinary hymn rack became a study in lights and shadows. Along the curving surface of the oak, dim reflections of stained-glass windows formed exotic and indescribably beautiful patterns.

Since that day that pew has never looked the same. Though it produced no soul-stirring message, an hour of relaxed attention opened a door to reveal never-suspected beauty in the very familiar.

Insistent on Expression

Regardless of the circumstances under which it emerges, a creative discovery brings with it a special dynamic. There is an urge to share what has been found. No incidental factor or aftermath, this factor is basic to illumination.

Habakkuk became possessed by consciousness of a challenge to hear Jehovah's message. But his sense of responsibility was social as well as personal. Early in his listening he was instructed: "Write the vision, and make it plain upon tables, that he may run that readeth it." (Hab. 2:2.)

More is involved than publicizing a message, however enlightening. Until the fruit of awareness is translated into words or other symbols, until some form (however ill-fitting) has been given the formless, revelation is not complete. Writing down the vision is integral to the vision itself.

It is true that no translation of experience into words can ever be adequate. Confronted by a demand to express the inexpressible, we cry, "O for a thousand tongues!" Trying to verbalize the soul's formless knowing of God we beg for help: "Come, Thou almighty King, help us Thy name to sing, help us to praise!"

Vivid personal discovery can be made public only with difficulty. Glimpses of God evoke sighs too deep for words. Yet we are given not merely a challenge but a divine imperative to write our visions and make them as plain as our skill with words will permit. The very process of attempting to find words with which to communicate our insights will enhance our awareness of fresh truth.

So one of the most important practices we can establish is that of giving expression to things seen and heard. Mechanical form of such translating and recording can vary widely. It may take any pattern from that of keeping a formal daily journal to random scribbling of notes on index cards.

It is not the form that matters; that is simply a technique, an outer shell. What counts is the establishment of a fixed habit of recording, in a fashion that suits your personality, those discoveries and insights that are themselves insistent upon expression.

6
Five Ways to Increase
the Value of Your Notes

EACH OF US NEEDS TO DEVELOP HIS OWN PATTERN OF RECORDING
fruits of heightened awareness. Whether to write full sentences
or simply words and phrases is a matter of individual preference.

Yet it is not enough to preserve ideas and impressions in casual
fashion. To write a vision in slipshod style is to do it injustice. In
order to make it plain so that he who runs may read, effort is
required. Therefore, this chapter is devoted to a number of specific disciplines for channeling your effort.

1. *Record insights without waiting for applications.*

On a hot Sunday afternoon I arrived in a city adjacent to a
permanent army post. Fifteen minutes of strolling revealed some
striking traits in the city's personality. Brief notes made on the
spot were dropped into the file with no idea of when or how
they would be used. Three years later, there came a request for
a talk on the church's responsibility to men in uniform. An intro-
duction was provided by polishing notes made with no idea of
when or how they would be used.

"Roll up your sleeves, mister."

Only the jerky way he puffed on his cigarette betrayed Johnny's
52

Look for ideas & not application. Apply the idea later.

nervousness. He pretended indifference as the swarthy, stolid woman shaved his arm with the detachment of long practice.

"Whatcha want on it?" she demanded.

There were plenty of choices. Seventy-five frames of tattoo art. Pay your money and take your pick. A nude mermaid. Or a rugged tombstone with the emblem, "In Memory of Mother." Even Christ with a crown of thorns.

Johnny, just turned eighteen, picked a military emblem. Aloud, he suggested that next pay day, he might come back and get a girl on the other arm. Right now, the insignia of his outfit would be O.K.

Two older soldiers paused to peer through the window.

"Somebody oughta tell the kid," one of them murmured. "Yeah, the goon," agreed his buddy.

If you wait until you expect to preach on problems of our military age, it will be too late to find firsthand material without great expenditure of time and effort. Gathering experiences wherever they are found without regard to use will pay off in time saved and vividness gained.

The actual writing of a sermon can be done at your desk. But construction of a message is distinct from accumulating its components. Many vigorous discoveries will come when you are relaxed, and not looking for specific ideas. Half-attention fosters entrance into the "night of awareness." In it, the mind is partially freed from denomination of conventional sets of meanings.

Be prepared, therefore, to verbalize your insights gained in such situations as

travel
    while shaving, brushing teeth, combing hair
      sun bathing
        during worship
          drifting off to sleep

immediately upon waking
  actually dreaming
    driving a car
      at the barber shop
        on the golf course

Unless captured on the spot and reduced to a memo while the moment of awareness remains vivid, even a thrilling discovery may be lost. In *Walden*, Thoreau records his chagrin at having failed to record an impression. "My thoughts have left no track, and I cannot find the path again," he confesses. After a futile effort to reconstruct the moment of illumination, he made this memo for his future guidance: "There never is but one opportunity of a kind." [1]

By acting on opportunities found without searching, your journal or notebook will come to hold much material that may never be used. This means that your deposits in the preaching bank will always exceed your withdrawals.

Here is a surplus item from my own inventory. Whether it will ever be used, I do not know, but it indicates the kind of notes that can be made quickly, on the spot, with at least a possibility of future utility:

Tiny country church on a spring Sunday. Old lady, heavy on her feet and wearing a flowered hat, has to be helped up plank steps. Toothless and wheezing, she explains she's been dragging for two years. But she has hobbled half a mile to 10:00 service, clutching a handful of jonquils which she puts in a fruit jar on top of the piano.

As the risk of belaboring the point, notice that even brief notes have potential for enriching some future message. If in the memory of imagination I should search for words to describe a faithful old woman bringing her splendid gift to a one-room frame church, I would fail to achieve the reality of the situation. This factor gives rise to a second principle.

2. _Make your notes specific and detailed._

Precise words which point to sensory experiences help create definite situations. Vague words which combine to form general statements are likely to depict only a fuzzy, lifeless situation. So it is helpful to record more details than you are likely to use:

Two days after Easter. 8:45 A.M. Clear blue sky, birds singing, warmth in air and green on land. At edge of yard, near street, a freshly tossed beer can. Machine imprinted can depicts doughty Falstaff swinging his tankard high—and lies, empty, just under a budding bush.

For those who have no eyes to see, even on the first day of Spring a can of beer beckons more invitingly than forsythia blossoms.

Abundant details make it possible to edit and cut when making use of a memo. Instead of having to use words that take up space but say nothing, material can be kept tight—hitting hard and commanding attention by conveying the listener to a specific situation.

A second advantage comes from feed-back effects. By training yourself to record specifics, your capacity to see them will grow. Instead of capturing general moods, you will note factors that produce them. Practice is required to see and record details that will provide a vivid description of a person or situation. Strive to notice colors, sizes, shapes, sounds, odors, and other specifics.

Striving for details will yield still another fruit. Even a vivid experience is likely to fade within a few weeks. If you attempt to recapture your own sense of involvement, details will help re-create the situation so it may be lived in memory. But if you have only a general impression, the best you are likely to achieve is a comment rather than a graphic description.

Early in my own keeping of a notebook, I made a two-line entry that gives no details. Hence no amount of effort will take me back to the scene to experience it vividly. Instead of a specific account that takes listeners where they can watch lust in action, the best I can manage is a reference to "the type of man who loiters in lingerie departments cutting his eyes at the displays."

Contrast that sketchy, nebulous, impersonal allusion with a memo that includes enough details to make the incident live:

Feb. 16. Flying Nashville to Cincinnati. Big plane—symbol of man's capacity to master the material world. Only two passengers in front of me. One, Marine captain. 220 lbs. Clean-cut. Small mole on right cheek. Four rows of combat ribbons. Fine example of clean-cut, vigorous American male. Wholly oblivious to surroundings, reading. For twenty minutes, continued to pore over March issue, Red Ryder comic book.

Not all situations are so simple or clear that salient features emerge without coaxing. Especially when dozens of strong stimuli rain on you in the space of an hour, there is danger that none will be retained. So a third principle applies to many situations.

3. View selectively; take a good look at a few things.

A traveling display of art replicas, sponsored by Life magazine, was featured at the St. Louis Art Museum for several weeks. Elaborate "illuminations" of fifty masterpieces, plus the ceiling of the Sistine Chapel, made up the costly exhibit.

56

My wife and I first visited the show on Friday afternoon. We kept pace with the traffic and checked off every item in forty minutes.

Three days later, we returned and spent half an hour with El Greco's "Burial of the Count of Orgaz." Then we read encyclopedia accounts for keys to symbolism of the painting, and found ourselves positively delighted to learn that a foreground character is the artist's son. After only three months we compared memories and found that both of us have more vivid impressions of the "Burial" than of all the hastily-glimpsed paintings together.

On a trip to the zoo it is a temptation to careen from cage to cage—especially if pulled by a six-year-old: "Quick, let's beat the crowd to the monkey house! Elephants aren't as big as people say, are they? Boy, they have hot chocolate at the concession stand today—I think. We'll pass the seal tank on the way. Come on! But we just can't leave without seeing the lions and the tigers and the birds."

Such a tour has its merits, of course. Pleasure in taking it is not to be discounted. But in terms of vivid impressions, greater returns will come from spending enough time to really see the leopard: his coloring, the way muscles play under his skin, the length of eye lashes, the manner in which his claws curl, the color and shape of his eye features, the depth and tone of his snarls.

As a member of a crowd, whether at the zoo or a more formal place of entertainment, you lose capacity to observe if you become completely caught up in the spirit of the place and try to see everything at once. In order to see a few things vividly instead of many things vaguely, it is necessary mentally to withdraw for an instant—to become an onlooker instead of a participant.

One of the most vivid scenes at an ice follies show was simulated underwater action. All girls wore fins and flippers. Some had full costumes covered with scaly sequins; others exhibited long tails that dragged the bottom as they "swam" upright.

Suddenly, bubbles began to erupt from waist-high ornaments on the ice. One of the first drifted to the left, where at the edge of the rink a boy of nine climbed on the rail and lunged to seize it. He grabbed triumphantly, then opened his hand to find it empty, as 3,500 adults chuckled.

Then bubbles began spurting crazily from the ceiling. All over the house, men, women, and children tried to grab them. As they drifted down, I was fascinated to note that a big two-inch bubble clearly reflected all eighteen overhead lights. Then I saw that a tiny half-inch one did the same. Weakening, I wet the tip of my index finger and gingerly reached up to catch a descending bubble—which burst on contact!

Brief reflection suggested that all life is like the scene at the ice follies. We are caught up in the excitement, devote ourselves to frantic striving for achievement. We climb on chairs and clamber over one another to grab prizes. Loot seized, we clutch it in our fists for what eternity's perspective reveals to be only the split second required for the bubble to burst.

4. *Analyze unusual experiences soon afterward.*

Try as we may, in some instances it is impossible to concentrate on a limited aspect of a complex situation. Especially in bizarre surroundings, it is hard for us to take our eyes from the woods to focus even briefly on one tree. Under such circumstances, it is profitable to abandon the struggle for insight, and to review the experience within a few hours.

Lucien Price says that that is how he captured the essence of long talks with Alfred North Whitehead. Recalling them after a lapse of time, he found their salient features more effectively than would have been possible from making reams of hasty notes.

From an experience of constant vivid impressions that last for two or three hours, your mind is likely to be so stuffed that you feel glutted. After a few hours some of the impressions fade. As mental digestion proceeds, memorable impressions grow clearer. Some descriptive details are lost. But if, after a day or two, you will devote half an hour to reliving a dynamic situation, you will discover things hardly noticed at the time.

For our minds are like fish. When they are really biting, we have to haul them out of the water so fast we hardly take a look at them. Later, at home or around a campfire, each individual beauty can be taken from the string, examined, and recorded.

Space forbids giving more than one example,. An afternoon at the State Fair was so filled with sights and sounds that it was virtually a vague oblong blur! Next day, however, many surface impressions faded and left a few incidents vivid in memory. Here are notes about one of them:

Sideshow, 25¢ for children and 35¢ for adults. Expected a gyp, but found it lively and entertaining. Dark-skinned woman, perhaps Syrian, "burned alive." Eight-foot-eight-inch Icelander exhibited.

Then leather-throated barker announced "special added attraction with slight additional cost." For 25¢, view "hospital delivery of a baby. It's the real thing, authentic, educational. Adults only, please. All under 16, kindly stand to one side." But many who looked 13,

14, even 12 years old, pressed up and handed him their quarters to march in unchallenged.

When you want his quarter badly enough, every boy is sixteen!

5. *Meditate on possible meanings.*

When examined from a number of perspectives, a given experience has potential for yielding more than one set of meanings. Search for such meanings and selection of the most significant ones can take place after an experience has been committed to journal or notebook. Given salient features, the question of "message" can be posed after the event.

Sometimes insights will come fully formed, shouting their messages. But in other instances, you will know you have been touched by life without quite knowing what to make of the incident. Such cases are fertile when approached with the certainty that they point to God and his ways with men.

The fruits of analysis are highly personal. They become social to the degree that my conclusion or yours speaks to others. So part of the analytical process is aimed at discovering insights applicable to men in general. It will be strange if the incident here shared fails to evoke in you some meanings I have overlooked in my thinking about it:

June 16. Driving into town of El Dorado. Stopped at service station for information: "Can you direct me to the Methodist Church?" Attendant stared. Maybe my southern accent, maybe the license on car, maybe my general appearance. No reply. Request repeated. He looked me up and down: "Why do you want to know?"

A good question. What is my motive for coming? To try to get a few dollars for the cause I represent? To bolster my own prestige? Or to break the bread of life to hungry men and women? Good question for those in any congregation. Why did you seek out this church today? What do you want: to have your prejudices reinforced, or to have the door jarred open? To sit comfortably for an hour and feel you have been religious for the week, or to be challenged to go out and live differently? Why do you want to know where the church is?

In your analysis of deep meanings to be found from casual incidents, the most effective single practice is daily use of the Scriptures. This matter is so central that it requires separate treatment.

7

Scripture's Lens Changes
All Seeing

GLASS IS THE MOST STRIKING COMMODITY OFFERED IN AN ANTIQUE shop. That is the case even when the range of displays runs from hat pins to wagon wheels and from Confederate money to flat irons.

Scripture affects our viewing of events in somewhat the same way that glass affects light.

Antique glass comes in many shapes: bowls, pitchers, lamps, tumblers, goblets, bottles, vases, mirrors. Scripture has taken shape through a variety of literary forms: history, poetry, folk wisdom, hymns, personal letters, prophetic witness, gospel narrative.

Glass may be blown, pressed, or cut. Frequently it is clear, but often it is tinted. No matter how it is shaped, regardless of the utilitarian function primary in the mind of its maker, glass transforms rays that pass through it or fall on it. Bending, twisting, reflecting, and splitting into component colors, glass adds dynamic and variety to light. So the glass-user does not live in a static universe with fixed appearance and meaning. Using now a lens and then a prism, now a clear mirror and then a tinted bottle, he can explore as many worlds as he has varieties of glass with which to enter them.

God's word as contained in the Scriptures includes a diversity of vessels. Their forms and functions dazzle our eyes. But surface differences cannot keep us from seeing fundamental traits common to all. Each segment of Scripture is like others in its power to transform our vision.

Rightly used, the Bible is the most potent and revealing lens the preacher may employ in his quest for larger vision. Let us therefore examine some useful and revealing ways to approach it.

1. *Search for personal enlargement.*

What you find in any experience is partly a fruit of the motive with which you enter it. It is one thing to search the Scriptures today to find a text on which to expound to others next Sabbath. It is quite a different thing to read in hope of gaining light with which to guide your own feet along your path today.

Over and over, the psalms echo a refrain of challenge: "Praise ye."

As a minister, I am particularly stirred by the pronoun. Injunctions to soul-possessing praise are not mine simply for ritual use in directing other men. They are addressed to me. In a sense, they are especially for my personal benefit.

God sheltered a people, inspired her poets, and preserved their witness in order that I should see the whole drama as coming to focus in me! God save me from using the Scriptures as "preaching material" from which to fashion messages for others. They must speak to me—and only so may I dimly echo to others what I have heard.

It is at the point of personal dynamic that values of using the Scriptures themselves are apparent. No matter how vivid and helpful they may be, devotional and critical studies are "secondhand" materials. They witness to what someone else has found.

To dwell continually with commentaries and expositions is to miss opportunities for firsthand meeting. "A Mighty Fortress Is Our God" can make the blood run faster. But to focus upon Luther's hymn to the exclusion of Ps. 46 is to forfeit an opportunity to light my candle at the fire which set the reformer's mind ablaze.

Partly as a result of emphasis on historical and literary criticism in theological seminaries, and partly because devotional guides flourish, many a seeker for God studies the Scriptures rather than studying life through them. Differences in results are profound.

My spectacles can be approached as objects of knowledge. If I should investigate them so, I would wish to be familiar with formulas that guided the grinder who fashioned lenses. It is significant that metal portions of the frames are of gold, 1/10 12 karat filled. Chemical composition of plastic ear pieces and method of manufacture could form the subject of long inquiry. But no degree of understanding the history and manufacture of spectacles has the same effect as that which comes from putting a pair of them before my eyes and viewing the world through them.

Used as instruments through which to look at life, the Scriptures transform our seeing. Personal enlargement is the primary goal; effects on preparation of messages for others are by-products of the personal search.

2. *Search while your mind is fresh.*

This lamp that Jehovah has provided for his anointed (Ps. 132:17) is no dead thing to be shined and placed on the trophy shelf. It must be held in the hand and pointed at immediate surroundings.

Maximum light for the day's journey comes from using the lamp before the sun is high.

After having partaken of the mystery of sleep, you rise with a hungry mind. Not yet crowded with concerns of the world, eager instead of weary, your early morning mind is a receptive vessel quite different from that of your late evening mind. A chapter of Isaiah read last night after a chaotic day left you unmoved. This morning the identical passage bristles with fresh meanings.

It is hard to enjoy a stack of buckwheat cakes and maple syrup after a breakfast of orange juice, oatmeal, sausage, toast and jelly, and coffee. Just so, it is hard to draw thrilling messages from Scripture after filling your mind with the morning newspaper, two or three phone calls, a stack of mail, list of appointments, and a conference with a disgruntled constituent. "Too late is better than never," but when reading for personal light, best results come from using the lamp with a receptive and uncluttered mind.

3. *Make use of brief intervals.*

Given a day oriented toward God by an early draught of living water, it is easy and natural to find later intervals for sipping. But should I always carry a Bible everywhere I go? It is not ordinarily convenient for us to take about with us a library of sixty-six volumes, even when printed on India paper and bound into a single Book. Besides, the appearance of the typical Bible brands it as somber, forbidding, and far removed from everyday life.

Scripture portions in lively format, in sizes convenient for keeping at hand, may prove one answer. Individual books of the Bible, printed in small paperback editions, are available at trifling cost from the American Bible Society.*

If you set out to feast on the riches of John's gospel for a period of six months, you may secure half a dozen copies for five cents each. One may be placed in the glove compartment of your car, another on a bedside table, a third in your pocket, and others distributed at spots where idle moments are likely to occur.

Besides transforming the quality of intervals that once were empty, the practice of turning to Scripture several times each day will prove more enlightening than one long session. For diverse situations and moods help evoke new insights. There must be constant interplay between Scripture and life if each is to reveal new significance in the other.

A dialectic process can be seen at work here. Each step upward on the ladder of Scripture provides leverage for a climb toward greater understanding in other areas. Meanwhile, each upward surge along the stairway of life gives a new perspective from which to view the message of the Book.

There is no escape from darkness and the need for illumination. Just as each twenty-four hour cycle sees both shadows and night, so in the daily movements of life there come perplexities and doubts. God has provided for these moments "a lamp unto my feet, and a light unto my path" that functions as a flashlight with a lifetime battery. Unlike man's lights, this one gets brighter the more it is used!

* Depositories are located at: 85 Walton Street, Altanta 3, Ga.; 310 N. Michigan Avenue, Chicago 1, Ill.; 2233 Bryan Street, Dallas 4, Texas; 450 Park Avenue, New York 22, N. Y.; 224 McAllister Street, San Francisco 2, Calif.

4. Seek meanings for which words are clumsy containers.

No one knows just how words serve to communicate meanings between men. This sublime capacity of creatures made in the image of God is the key to social achievements that form "civilization." But in all searching for illumination, remember that words are simply vessels for meanings—not the meanings that are sought.

Augustine sounds a universal note when he yearns for such divine grace that "the inner parts of Thy words may be opened unto me as I knock." [1] Chesterton compares the grinding power of the Bible's words with that of grain-crushing stones and insists that "those who can read them simply enough will feel as if rocks had been rolled upon them." [2]

Dynamic encounter with meanings that gripped men before they put their insights into words is not easily come by. It requires that we stand where the ancient writer stood and look at life through his eyes. There must be imaginative participation in the discoveries that evoked verbal reports.

"Empathy" is perhaps the best label we have to point at this interior process. "The entrance of thy words giveth light; it giveth understanding unto the simple." (Ps. 119:130.) In a situation that includes an inquiring mind, light can be transforming. Without combining with any ingredients, light reveals (or creates?) relationships: colors, sheens, perspective, reflections, glosses, and shadows. To recognize these marvels is one thing; to reduce light's effects to a formula is quite another!

Just so with the transforming work of Scripture. It can be vividly experienced, but not adequately described for understanding by those who have not experienced. When a writer describes a particular mood, full understanding is reserved for those who have felt it.

Augustine was reared in a culture where "slavery" was not simply a word in the dictionary, but a living institution. At least half a dozen times in his writings, he declares that only those who have been slaves can fully understand when preachers speak of bondage. And the author of The Imitation of Christ insists that Christ's passion remains an empty concept to those who have not suffered deeply.

Searching for enlargement requires that you repudiate the contemporary emphasis on rapid reading. That is valid only when you seek information. When you read in meditative fashion, speed is more likely to inhibit than to foster the flow of meanings.

You can eat lima beans rapidly—for calories. When this is your goal, heap up your fork and move it quickly from plate to lips.

But if you wish really to experience lima beans, place two or three in your mouth before anything else has been tasted. Slip them between teeth and lips, then move them where their size and smoothness can be felt as the tongue pushes them first against the roof of your mouth and then against the back of your teeth. Squeeze one between tongue and teeth. Then place another between your teeth and crush it. Tasting and feeling in this way for only ninety seconds, you will experience lima beans in "depth" that cannot be gained from years of gulping.

Whether dealing with food for the body or with the bread of life, each encounter increases potential for new discoveries. To spend a day or two with a single paragraph, turning to it many times for brief consideration from diverse angles, is to invite a stream of vital meanings. Each discovery throws light on its context; the flow of insight is not linear, but takes place as a "field phenomenon."

A two-day feast on the riches of Ps. 84 brought personal discovery of meanings in this sequence of verse fragments: 2a, 2b, 10a, 10b, 3, 11a, 11c, 4a, 1, 4b, 7a, 8, 2b, 5a.

It came as a thrilling discovery to recognize from verse 11a that because God is a sun and a shield, he is above all our logical categories. God is not either/or, but both/and. At one and the same time, he gives out blinding heat and serves as a shield to protect his own from burning! In himself, God wholly transcends all the neat categories men have set up. No affirmation about him is exhaustive or final—for its opposite may be equally valid!

Lacking combined effects of ideas evoked by verses 2a, 2b, 10a, 10b, and 3, it would not have been possible to seize upon that precise insight from verse 11a. Slow, meditative searching yields much more fruit than hasty skimming over long sections.

5. *Employ a variety of versions and translations.*

In its entirety, the Bible consists of verbal reports and interpretations. Men who have encountered God use the words of common speech to express what they have found. Part of the work of translation is finding synonyms for ancient words, and arranging them in sentences. Both the choice of a modern equivalent for a biblical original and the way it is set into its context may affect reactions of readers.

For example, the King James Version challenges us to have patience in order to possess our souls (Luke 21:19). In the Revised Standard Version, the attitude that is mentioned is "endurance." And J. B. Phillips discards both these formal terms to have Jesus promise: "Hold on, and you will win your souls!"

While the three translations are equivalent, they are far from identical. Any one of them may catch attention and shed light, though the other two have been read without arousing interest. Exclusive use of a particular translation can easily lead us to focus upon words rather than upon the meanings for which words are vehicles. Whether in Hebrew, Aramaic, Latin, Shakespearean English, or modern American idiom, words have no sacredness in themselves. It is their function as potent pointers to God that is significant.

So treated, familiar words of a favorite translation may reveal new light at every reading. Again, the vividness that comes from rephrasing in fresh language may cause a time-honored passage to break open and yield deep meaning that was never before grasped. It is profitable, therefore, both to read from your favorite translation and to turn at intervals to less familiar ones.

Many readers of the Bible restrict their explorations to works that are accepted in their own communion. Some light new lamps in the forms of versions endorsed by other branches of Christendom. For that reason the following list cuts across conventional lines and suggests a wide variety of translations and versions:

The Authorized (King James) Version, a Church of England translation first issued in 1611.

Ronald A. Knox, *The Old Testament* (2 vols.); *The New Testament* (New York: Sheed & Ward). Msgr. Knox was an English Catholic of this century.

George M. Lamsa, *The Holy Bible from Ancient Eastern Manuscripts* (Philadelphia: A. J. Holman Co.). Translated from the Peshitta, authorized Bible of the church of the East.

James Moffatt, *The Old Testament* (2 vols.); *The New Testa-*

ment (New York: Harper & Brothers). Dr. Moffatt was a twentieth-century Scottish theologian and historian.

The New Testament, translated from the Latin Vulgate (Paterson, N. J.: St. Anthony Guild Press, 1941). Official Roman Catholic translation.

The New Testament in Basic English, ed. S. H. Hooke (New York: E. P. Dutton & Co.). "Basic" employs a vocabulary of less than 1,000 words.

The New Testament in Modern English, tr. J. B. Phillips (New York: The Macmillan Company).

The Revised Standard Version, translated by Western Protestants and issued 1946 and 1952.

J. M. P. Smith and Edgar J. Goodspeed, *The Complete Bible: An American Translation* (Chicago: The University of Chicago Press). Employs the American rather than the English language.

Hugh J. Schonfield, *The Authentic New Testament.* (New American Library, Mentor Book). Translated from the Greek; rich in allusions to non-Christian influences.

Richard Francis Weymouth, *The New Testament in Modern Speech.* (New York: Harper & Brothers).

Kenneth S. Wuest, *An Expanded Translation of the Greek New Testament.* (Grand Rapids, Eerdmans Publishing Company, 1958). A transliteration rather than a word-for-word translation.

6. *Conserve insights and discoveries.*

Mechanics of recording and preserving the flow of meanings will vary according to personality. Some men prefer a journal or notebook. Others favor use of index cards or a loose-leaf system. Preferences for manner of recording will run all the way from disconnected phrases to long, polished paragraphs.

Experiments will soon indicate what method of notation suits you. It is not the style of recording that matters, but adoption of some practice to conserve those discoveries that are revealed by Scripture's lens.

Inevitably many of them will be so personal that they have little social significance. Perhaps no more than ten per cent—or one per cent—will ever be used in writing sermons. But accumulation of a mass of notes eliminates the problem of searching for ideas and materials. Instead of struggling for a glimmer of light, the preacher with more material than he can use has just one problem: selecting from many competing ideas, each of which clamors for interpretation!

Bernard of Clairvaux expressed the matter for all time. Counseling preachers in language as appropriate to the twentieth century as the twelfth, he urged:

"If you are wise, therefore, you will show yourself a tank, and not a pipe. For a pipe pours out as fast as it takes in; but a tank waits until it is full before it overflows, and so communicates its surplus without loss to itself. We have all too few such tanks in the Church at present, though we have pipes in plenty.[3]

8

Paths to Discovery Through
Scripture's Power

AT A COLLEGE CHAPEL SERVICE, A VISITING MINISTER SPOKE ON
"Providence." Among those exposed to his words was a freshman in a plaid sport shirt who sat in the next-to-last row. During
most of the hour, he concentrated on a workbook entitled *Successful Adjustment in College*. He paused in his scribbling only
for the closing prayer and hymn.

For that freshman, analysis of Providence was pushed aside
because of preoccupation with adjustment to his present situation—college. Much the same thing can happen to a minister
who becomes absorbed with building up his congregation, making a record, and winning tangible results that reveal his leadership.

Scripture offers a corrective to this and other wanderings; and
it helps keep life so oriented that our sense of destination has
profound effects on all our messages.

1. *Our spiritual destination is emphasized.*

Within the realm of the material, we continually experience
twoness in oneness. Though the universe is coherent, its components are divided into pairs of categories: day, night; male, fe-
male; living, dead; and the like.

It is a fundamental message of Scripture that there is another

73

order of dualism whose nature is dimly hinted by such concepts as heaven, earth; Creator, creature; eternity, time. Monumental literary works of Christendom have been shaped by acute consciousness of this dividedness in the nature of things and of the primacy of the spiritual destination. Diverse as they are in some respects, *The City of God*, *The Divine Comedy*, and *Pilgrim's Progress* are alike in their emphasis on the priority of heaven's claims over those of earth.

Every airline ticket counter is equipped with scales. These serve to test all passengers. But it is not the passenger who steps upon the scales; instead, his baggage is weighed.

Here is a parable of taking flight for our eternal destination. It is the amount of baggage—in the form of concern for self and material things—that must be weighed. Wise travelers go over their suitcases frequently and take out gear that contributes to excess weight. For those of us who preach as well as for those whom we challenge from the pulpit, values underscored in the Bible provide standards by which to decide what to throw away.

One who is striving to travel without excess baggage, and has been stirred to sensitivity by Scriptural challenges, may stumble on transforming insights in unexpected places.

Among the cultural institutions of the Midwest is the "country auction." When a householder dies, his heirs bring together all his personal effects. They hire an auctioneer, advertise, and invite the public to come and buy.

One such auction, held on a frosty December morning, offered the usual conglomeration of belongings. There were four horses, twelve cows, and thirty sheep. Two wagon beds were piled high with tools, scrap metal, and rolled wire. Antique collectors nudged one another at the sight of a thirty-gallon copper kettle in which apple butter had been made the previous season. There was a brass bed adorned with a frayed canopy, and four bundles of used coat hangers.

A table piled high with glassware and bric-a-brac included a 2"x3" folding metal picture frame with one side empty and the other holding a tintype of Grandma Mueller. There was no doubt of her identity, for a relative saw the picture and commented about it.

Viewed from the perspective of Scripture's fundamental emphasis upon our spiritual destination, the country auction points to a basic truth. One day soon—very soon, as the cosmic clock ticks—I will be called to appear before the Father. Relatives will hire an auctioneer and set up a hot dog stand in the tool shed, with root beer and coffee for the nice people who'll buy the apple butter kettle for $14.75 and grandma's tintype for a dime.

No matter what, I can take nothing with me. Why bother with a mad scramble to accumulate trinkets, when it is only seconds before every piece will go to strangers or to cousins who've held out a few choice pieces from the sale? Working for the church is by no means the same thing as working for God through the church. No matter what, I can keep nothing—not even a major honor of the church, not even a list of distinguished achievements, not even a catalogue of quotas met and exceeded, not even an inventory of the hours spent in the Lord's work. No other goal is so significant as that of better understanding what God says to me, in order that I may stride toward a house not built with hands.

2. *Eyesight and hearing are continually sharpened.*

Two hours spent with art masterpieces will reval new dimensions of light because it is glimpsed through the eyes of great painters. Given acute vision by the contagion of art, the world is temporarily transformed. Light from the afternoon sun falls on a glass in the museum restaurant. Only an ordinary tumbler it is, empty except for two ice cubes; but viewed with heightened sensitivity to light, it glows with marvels. Light-showered glass and ice are fluid, dazzling, and evocative—so profound that no man can plumb their deepest meanings. Words cannot fully describe them; no pigments can depict them in all their grandeur.

Every encounter with a work of art affects the viewer's capacity to see both art and life. Doors are opened by observing how Monet is fascinated by water on a lily pond, how El Greco handles colors and shapes, how Pierre Bonnard portrays nebulous but vital children in a flower garden without showing any actual lines.

To look for half an hour through the eyes of an artist-creator is a growth-inducing experience. At least for a time everything that one sees is viewed in quietly exalted fashion. Just so, every encounter with Scripture has a carry-over effect on all situations. Instead of being dull and meaningless, ordinary events are explosive with cues and signs that point to God.

Driving south on U.S. 45, the traveler who approaches Siegel, Illinois, finds it very much like other towns of the region. There is no skyline in the sense that it is a feature of cities. Instead, there are just three familiar outlines: a grain elevator, a water tank, and a church steeple.

Nothing of interest here—until one dons the spectacles of the Fourth Gospel and gains heightened awareness of the bread of life and the living water. So viewed, this village profile is not dull

76

and ordinary. It shouts to every passerby: "Why do you hurry past? Linger and grow wise!"

Grain elevator, water tank, and church steeple. Bread, water, and spirit. Each is as basic as the other. Patterns of culture and styles of architecture change, but man's fundamental needs are fixed.

In somewhat different fashion, an encounter with an aged stranger ceases to be trivial, and become momentous when Scripture transforms the scene. There he is, an old gentleman whom you've never seen before, alone and sleeping noisily in the lobby of a small-town hotel. His open mouth reveals a grey tongue; a hearing aid and a cane lie beside his chair. Big skin cancers blotch his nose, neck, and cheeks. Nothing here except a somewhat nauseating spectacle made by a man you'll never see again, and with whom you will exchange no word.

No, that is not right. For without pausing in his snoring, he has spoken:

Listen, friend! There are things more important than social security and annuity rates. Stop fretting about how you will live when you are old. If you attain unto many years, "yet is their strength labour and sorrow." It is not the duration of your life that matters—but its destination. Where do you go in such a hurry? Is what you are doing today really more important than my sleeping?

3. *Life is flooded with delight.*

It is futile to approach the cultivation of interaction between Scripture and life as though this were simply a worthy task. Regarded as an aspect of your work, exercises in self-enlargement could be as dreary as any other work. The journey must be run for the sheer joy of running.

77

Like other complex states of personality, abounding joy is beyond analysis. C. S. Lewis confessed himself to be *Surprised by Joy*. In doing so, he spoke for all who have attempted to indicate just how delight takes possession of the self.

Though mysteries abound, this much is clear: conscious participation in personal enlargement is a source of much profound pleasure. So viewed, parenthood may well offer the apex of human delight.

On a quite different level, we gain pleasure from solving puzzles and mastering skills. To learn to sing a hymn, write an epigram, or recite a poem is to participate in creative outreach and thereby to enter joy. Similar rewards result from coming into genuine meeting with a stranger and finding a fresh interpretation of a familiar gospel text.

It is great fun to discover fresh insights, even on a trivial scale. So there is a special kind of delight linked with meditation on the law of the Lord.

Any common situation can become more challenging and rewarding than a crossword puzzle or mystery novel. Here are the ingredients of an incident; for the moment, they convey no message. But I am sure that if I could look through the lens of Scripture, I would discover profound truth.

That announcement at the rodeo, for example: "We have a lost boy at the platform. He has big brown eyes, and he says his name is Joe. Mother or father, please come claim him!" After a brief interlude: "Another child at the platform, ladies and gentlemen. This one's Susie Smith. She says she's not lost—but her mother and father are!"

That quip is good for a chuckle—and a closer look. Really, who is lost in this situation? Is Susie lost, or are her parents?

Such a query makes the matter too simple. To be lost is to be in a state of separation. To be found is to be in a relationship. As with children at the sports arena, so with men and women in God's world. Lostness is a state of separation from the Father; salvation is a state of conscious relatedness. So viewed, salvation is not so much a once-for-all rescue as it is a continual participation in a state of connectedness.

How delightful to stumble on such an insight at the rodeo! What a good day it has been, for it has brought fresh understanding of a central mystery! How good it is to be alive in a world whose shelves are loaded with fascinating meanings to be gained for the price of looking!

4. *Sense of message is heightened.*

Regardless of its nature that which has just been discovered or revealed is likely to be viewed with zest.

An exciting new book sets your mind on fire. What do you do? You refer to it in formal public messages and casual conversation; you buttonhole friends and exchange only a few sentences before revealing your enthusiasm: "Say, I've just finished the most fascinating book."

It is the function of novelists and poets, painters and cartoonists, photographers and essayists, preachers and prophets to make public those fresh truths they have discovered. Any man gains dynamic if he consistently participates in creative outreach. This truth you proclaim today is offered with zeal and persuasiveness because it is still shiny with newness and precious because you found it.

The mastery of techniques is not enough. This may give you capacity to please an audience, but is not likely to yield dynamic

79

with which to move men deeply. It is more important clumsily to have something to say than cleverly to say nothing.

At the Museum of Science and Industry in Chicago, the telephone room is one of the most popular exhibits. One display invites visitors to speak into a phone to "hear yourself as others hear you."

So many persons were attracted to this exhibit one afternoon that adults and children alike stood in line waiting their turn at the "magic" red telephone. But one after another—adults even more frequently than children—those who reached their turn hummed and hawed and flushed when the light flashed for them to speak. One nineteen-year-old with his girl on his arm stood grinning and silent as three times the recorded message invited him to speak into the phone.

It is useless to have all the technical equipment without a sense of message! Vigor and authority will overcome limitations of any medium of communication. Constant intake of insights and discoveries will add dynamic to all communication. When oriented toward the Creator, listening brings power that makes men give heed. As translated by Ronald Knox, an obscure Palestinian seer dared to demand: "let the whole world give audience, and all the world contains!" (Mic. 1:2.)

On lower levels there is at least a chance of reducing the number of sleepers on any given Sunday morning when you speak with the urgency of having discovered fresh truths!

5. *Literary style is gradually transformed.*

Our dialects and brogues give vague clues and sometimes broad hints as to the region in which we learned to talk. These influences are not usually noticed during the period in which they are affecting our ways of moving tongue and lips.

In the same fashion the literary heritage with which a person dwells is sure to have subtle but lasting influence upon his style. Exclusive attention to the daily paper will tend to modify your speech in the direction of "journalistic" style, even if you never consciously strive to meet the standards suggested by Rudolph Flesch. After spending just three hours at the Ballet Russe, you may find yourself tempted to join uninhibited children who spin and pirouette on tiptoe while making their way to the parking lot!

Gregory the Great once described the Bible as "the loveliest thing there is." He who dwells with that loveliness will have some of it rub off on him.

The fragrance of bacon clings to the hands for two or three hours after frying it; the perfumes of encounter with God through the Scriptures have equally powerful but much more significant effects. Over a period of years mere reading of the Bible will affect your vocabulary and usage more profoundly than any course of study in techniques of putting words together.

9
Emotional Factors Bend
All Seeing

SCRIPTURE STRESSES THE DIVINE IMPERATIVE THAT WE CULTIVATE awareness. It is not enough to praise Jehovah in stereotyped ways. He demands that we use all our resources in discovering fresh channels through which to enter into dialogue, praise, and witness.

"O sing unto the Lord a new song!"

Response to this challenge requires purposeful use of emotion, both in our search for messages and in making public those we find.

Folk psychology, preserved in the form of proverbs and sayings, has always recognized that our total outlook is affected by emotion. As the French put it, "Every bird likes its own nest best." Peasants of Siberia witness to the transforming power of hope by saying that "In the land of hope, there is never any winter." If you look at the world through rose-colored glasses, it seems quite different than it does when you suffer from an attack of blues!

Emotion is to the mind as a kaleidoscope is to the eye. Slight changes in the instrument provide an abundance of rich new patterns. To enter a transformed world you have only to move from fear or rage into trust or love.

Far from being an appendage to thought, emotion is a major variable in all seeing and knowing. Coleridge held that "deep thinking is obtainable only by a man of deep feeling." [1] Wordsworth's great *Prelude* is simply a composite of reports about the way feelings bring new insight.

Analyzing their capacity to discover beauty and truth, many artists and musicians have insisted that reason must actually be subordinate. Picasso goes so far as to describe an artist as "a receptacle for emotions that come from all over the place: from the sky, from the earth, from a scrap of paper, from a passing shape, from a spider's web." [2] In *A Midsummer Night's Dream* Shakespeare declared that emotions of lovers and madmen give them power to apprehend "more than cool reason ever comprehends."

Logic can bolster, but not create belief. Only emotion is powerful enough to set men seeking new goals with such force that discoveries are inevitable. It has several direct effects upon seeing, listening, and understanding.

1. *Emotion narrows the attention.*

Gripped by an absorbing passion, a seeker readily overlooks many things other men consider important. Everything encountered is weighed in terms of its significance in relation to the life-directing goal.

That is why Paul counsels against marriage. He who takes a wife must pay attention to her needs and wants, while the man attached only to God can be "without carefulness" (I Cor. 7:32). Holy carelessness causes all other concerns to shrink into insignificance because of a single loyalty. This is the carelessness of one who runs without waiting to be sure his shoes will hold out for the journey.

In Bunyan's dynamic allegory of the search for life, Christian meets an evangelist and is brought under conviction. He realizes he must use all his energy to flee from the City of Destruction. He has gone only a short way before his wife and children see what he is doing and cry for him to return.

Christian hears them call, and is torn between conflicting loyalties. But he puts his fingers in his ears and takes up his flight, crying: "Life! life! Eternal Life!" [3]

Emotion plays a potent role in our seeing and understanding. Wrapping supple fingers over eyes of the mind, she cuts off those signals which, if heeded, would interfere with the dominant quest. Attention is narrowed almost as though physical changes were made.

In attempting to take leave of a blind man, it is useless to twist in your chair, glance repeatedly at the clock, or sit upright in a preliminary move toward rising. We constantly use such signals without thought. But they have no effect on a man who cannot see nonverbal hints to close the conversation. That is why it is hard to break away from a blind man or from one who has eyes, but is preoccupied with an idea.

2. *Negative emotions inhibit discovery.*

Rage, jealousy, scorn, despair, doubt, vexation, ennui, dejection, and other negative emotional states restrict our outlook. Clues that shout for attention may be ignored when the mind is dominated by such a mood. Jews who questioned the man healed at the pool of Bathesda were so indignant at work on the Sabbath that they were blind to the marvelous fact that a long-time cripple was standing on his feet talking with them.

When in a state of petulance even a great poet may be blind

84

to evidence of goodness, beauty, and purity. Ronald Knox translates the confession of Ps. 31:9 to read: "Vexation has dimmed my eyes."

Much the same thing can be said of any man absorbed with plans to gain revenge or attack others; "He that hateth his brother is in darkness, and walketh in darkness, and knoweth not whither he goeth, because that darkness hath blinded his eyes" (I John 2:11). Grief that is acute to the point of bitterness, when viewed in restrospect may lead us to recognize that emotion made us foolish and dull—more like beasts than men (Ps. 73:22).

Even after having been led by Jehovah across a desert, there were some among the children of Israel who could not enter Canaan "because of unbelief" (Heb. 3:19).

Such is the nature of doubt that it prevents entrance into any land of promise. To the man who doubts his wife's fidelity, effective marriage is a strange and distant land. Dimly glimpsed sometimes, it is forever barred so long as skepticism persists. Those bits of testimony that support a different conclusion remain invisible while suspicion clouds the eyes.

Implications for our task as preachers are stupendous. That day spent in a negative state is not likely to yield valid insights.

At worst, it can lead to an explosion. Many a man has gathered preaching material in anger and proceeded to blister his congregation—only to repent, too late, of having selected evidence while looking through partly closed eyes. Judgments reached under a blinding influence must be regarded as suspect, to be reexamined in a different mood.

At best a period of negative emotion will prove sterile. There is little value in searching for fresh messages from God so long as one is dominated by a mood that cuts off communication. Before there can be a flood of discovery, a creative emotional state must be entered through repentance, discipline, searching of the Scriptures, and worship.

3. *Expectancy reveals clues.*

It is neither accidental nor incidental that the gospel record puts great stress upon expectancy. An eagerly watchful disciple will discover evidence that stolid folk fail to notice.

As early as the fourteenth century this matter was clearly expressed by the German mystic, Meister Eckhart. Those who long to see the Lord, he said, are "always ready to find him in whatever comes along; however strange it may be, they always think he might be in it." [4]

A common proverb declares that what we seek with eagerness we readily find. Hostility of a mother-in-law may lead her to overlook the charm of a bride, while adoration of his beloved causes the bridegroom to exult over traits that wedding guests do not even notice. Martin Luther entered a new phase of his spiritual development through an experience in which a theological phrase was central. His emotional involvement led to subjective magnification whenever he found clues pointing to "justification by faith." So he discovered supporting evidence in situations that seemed barren to less fervent eyes. Old and familiar books yielded fresh meanings because he read them with new ardor.

4. *Positive emotions enhance capacity to see.*

A wife sets out to drive back to her girlhood home because of an emergency. The husband, who is eagerly hopeful of getting a message, is given a polarized mind. All signs point in one direction—late word from his beloved. Approaching footsteps are

86

heard from far away. Perhaps it is a messenger with a telegram! Every ring of the telephone is a signal to scramble for the receiver. At last, she has reached a place where she can call!

To the degree that we succeed in becoming aflame for God, our power to discover evidence and supporting illustrations is magnified. Eagerness to know God fosters creative capacity in a way not possible from cultivation of skills and techniques that lack emotional drive.

Ardent expectation contributes to the state Evelyn Underhill describes as so heightened that "each blade of grass seems fierce with meaning, and becomes a well of wondrous light." [5] Though too fiercely individual to accept orthodox religion, Walt Whitman lived in a state of magnified sensitivity during the period he gathered insights for *Song of Myself*. As a result, he discovered divine marvels everywhere:

I believe a leaf of grass is no less than the journey-work of the stars.
And the pismire is equally perfect, and a grain of sand, and the egg
    of the wren.
And the tree-toad is a chef-d'œuvre for the highest,
And the running blackberry would adorn the parlors of heaven,
And the narrowest hinge in my hand puts to scorn all machinery,
And the cow crunching with depress'd head surpasses any statue,
And a mouse is miracle enough to stagger sextillions of infidels.

Whether it persists for extended periods or brief interludes, so long as such an emotional state affords unusual sensitivity we can rejoice with Whitman:

I see something of God each hour of the twenty-four, and each
    moment then,

In the faces of men and women I see God, and in my own face in
    the glass,
I find letters from God dropt in the street, and every one is sign'd by
    God's name.[6]

Consciousness of a single clearly defined goal, that of reaching
the Father's house, is a major ingredient in the state of ecstasy.
Data ignored or discarded under other circumstances may evoke
a "new song of praise" when the soul is oriented toward a haven
for which it yearns.

One evening in late March, I checked into a hotel. Two
cards were displayed on the desk. The green one warned, "No
overnight parking in the business district." That was a routine
message, and it stirred no response. Under some circumstances,
little heed would have been given the red card which inquired:
"Are you planning to make this city your permanent home? If
so, please call the welcome committee of the Chamber of Com-
merce."

This time, however, I was on my way home. After an absence
of two weeks, this was my last night on the road. Tomorrow I
would reach the destination that absorbed all my attention and
on which my longing was focused. So an otherwise meaningless
card suddenly became explosive with meaning. I re-read its message and laughed aloud. Then I broke into song. As nearly as I
can reconstruct it, the tune must have been approximately that
of "Swing Low, Sweet Chariot." But the words were my own:

"No-o-o-o, no, no-o-o-o. Praise the Lord Jehovah, I'm on my
way home. Yes, Lord, I'm on my way ho-o-o-me! I'm just
a-spending the night. I'll be leaving here tomorrow. For I'm on
the way to my home!"

5. Emotion provides power for action.

Paul repudiated all floundering and insisted that he was deliberately striving for the prize of life. "I do not run aimlessly." (I Cor. 9:26 R.S.V.)

Actually there is no way to stagger or flounder with speed! You can walk in zigzag fashion or amble uncertainly. It is possible to plod along in wavering fashion. But the speed of running requires a precise path. To the degree that we succeed in recognizing one clear goal, we gain the capacity so to center our striving that every tiny clue is charged with significance for the race.

No degree of intellectual understanding alone can yield the dynamic of a soul charged with deep emotion. One who knows, but does not feel, lacks power. George Santayana said of such a person, "The truth, though he may frigidly assent to it, leaves him weary and cold." [7]

Chrysostom urged that all who love God should pay tribute to Hannah, the mother of Samuel. For he pointed out that her fervent prayers for a son were driven home by a flood of tears—while most of us "yawn while we pray for a kingdom!" [8]

Regardless of whether your goal is a new sermon, a poem, or a prayer, creative enterprise requires fervor. In his *Journal* for September 2, 1851, Thoreau put the matter in this fashion:

We cannot write well or truly but what we write with gusto. The body, the senses, must conspire with the mind. Expression is the act of the whole man, that our speech may be vascular. The intellect is powerless to express thought without the aid of the heart and liver and of every member.[9]

Jesus' healing of the woman with an issue of blood (Matt.

89

9:20-22) is in a class by itself. There was no request on her part, no exchange of words with the Master. In almost surreptitious fashion, she touched his garment—and was made whole. An event that to the casual observer seemed incidental was a point of transformation for the emotion-charged one. For her, so much hope and courage were poured into the groping reach for Jesus' garment that the situation was explosive. Her emotion created a symbolic moment with great dynamic—for her, and her alone. Those who did not share her expectancy were not prepared to receive its fruits.

Ambrose insisted that eager haste on the part of the shepherds was a factor in their discovery of the Christ child. "None came seeking Christ in sloth," he declared.[10] Whether searching for clues that lead to Bethlehem's manger or casting about for convincing and moving material in which to clothe next Sunday's sermon, emotional commitment is a source of power that has neither equal nor substitute.

10

Some Ways to Put Emotion
to Work

It is a hard lesson that Jesus teaches when he tells us: "This is the work of God, that ye believe on him whom he hath sent" (John 6:29).

No matter how often we hear that lesson, we find it difficult to understand that emotion-charged believing is the chief form of "work" in God's service. It is much easier to center on building programs and annual reports!

Because complex intangibles are involved, there are no easy formulas for use of emotion in discovery and witness. A few broad hints may have suggestive value.

1. *Cultivate recognition of personal danger.*

Even in lives oriented toward secular values, crisis fosters sensitivity. Clues ignored in times of complacency may loom to significance during periods of danger.

That is why spiritual law has an essential role even in the climate of Christian freedom. Symbolized and summarized in the Ten Commandments, the law serves to convict us all. For none can keep the letter of the law, to say nothing of its spirit. Law makes demands too great for human strength. So it becomes a sentence of death to each of us.

Vividly recognized, this death sentence creates tension. It is here that law functions as the great awakener. Condemned men are alert to every scrap of evidence that can be used in seeking a pardon. Vision and hearing are sharpened by crisis.

This factor contributes to battlefield moods that bring insights such as those described earlier. A major fruit of feeding on Scripture is a growing sense of involvement in spiritual battles whose issues are cosmic. Any day in which I recognize the need for rescue, my capacity to discover help is magnified. It is the perpetual "fear and trembling" of Paul that kept him uniquely sensitive to whispers from God.

Before emerging as a powerful leader, Peter passed through the eye-opening valley of the shadow of spiritual death. For the rest of his life, whenever he felt comfortable he had only to remember a servant girl's questions in order to recover a sense of guilt. Any day, any hour can bring recognition of failure and of sure condemnation in the judgment. Once entered, such a mood brings eagerness for rescue and acute sensitivity to divine messages.

2. *Frequently enter the mood of experiment.*

Almost any activity can stir the emotions the first few times it is pursued. Soon the sharp edge of newness wears off, and participation ceases to be an adventure. Habit dulls the senses; capacity to see and hear is reduced.

On my first plane trip, my whole system of perceiving was tuned to high pitch. My fingers were clumsy—almost numb—as they pressed against the buckle of my seat belt. My heart bolted when the pilot's voice came over the loudspeaker: "Observe the 'No Smoking' sign when it appears." Clearly, this was a precaution against igniting aviation gasoline in case we failed to clear the runway—an event that seemed altogether likely.

As the motors began throbbing and the plane thrust my body into a pattern of heavy vibrations, sweat broke out on my forehead. I gripped both arm rests with hands tense, and tried to look casual as a seatmate climbed past me. Every change in the sounds of the motors, each minor jolt, all the flashings of lights and making of announcements registered vivid impressions that day.

But after only half a dozen flights, I found myself all but oblivious to such signals.

In order to enter vividly into a familiar experience and observe aspects usually ignored, it is necessary to adopt the experimental mood. Recapture a degree of the expectancy that marked your first instance of participation. Deliberately seek to look and listen and feel from the perspective of one who is undertaking this adventure with eager uncertainty. So entered, any commonplace experience will provide a shower of impressions.

3. *Play the role of observer as well as participant.*

During deep emotion, it is difficult to notice specific factors that contribute to the mood. Fear can so dominate my mind that I am conscious only of being afraid, and cannot list or describe components of the situation.

In order to communicate about acute fear it is necessary to depict some of its aspects. This means that in order to re-create an emotion-charged situation I must step out of it mentally and become an onlooker instead of a principal.

Miguel de Unamuno makes it axiomatic that a change of perspective must take place as a prelude to creativity. "Great art,"

93

he says, "can only flourish in the temperate zone of the passions, on the return journey from the torrid." [1]

That is, if you would move men you must first be moved yourself.

When on the return journey from a mood of extraordinary intensity, you need to observe specific features of the terrain in order to describe it to others. Schelling suggested that the secret of true poetry is found only by those who succeed in being "drunk and sober not in different moments but at one and the same moment." [2] The making of descriptive notes may have to be deferred until emotion has relaxed its grip.

When my older son broke his arm, I hurried with him in search of a doctor. Though the boy was calm, the sight of his twisted forearm affected me so greatly that I blundered three blocks off course in driving to a familiar address.

At the clinic we were ushered into the fracture room. A nurse, casual from many experiences, attached wire stalls to Webb's thumb and forefinger. She adjusted a pulley, then hung an eight-pound weight so it would gradually pull the twisted arm into position.

When the surgeon came, the novocaine injection proved less frightening than I had expected. Then the doctor selected a big syringe with a long, flexible needle. He pressed it into the shattered wrist and slowly drew out blood—darkly red.

It was then that nausea began to mount within me. My head grew warm and the tips of my fingers throbbed faintly. They seemed stiff and enlarged. My heart pounded audibly. All outside noises seemed to come faintly from a distance. My extremities were far, far away. Speaking thickly, I muttered that I was getting hot and managed to fumble out of my coat. By a supreme effort I concentrated on the wallpaper pattern sufficiently to keep from fainting. But it was not until an hour later, released from the grip of a soul-dominating mood, that I could recall some of the sensory cues that contributed to it.

More than other men, we ministers have opportunity for enlargement through moving emotional experiences. Emotion generated in a preaching mission or a parish tragedy can provide the mind with powerful new instruments that yield fresh insights. But we are handicapped by our tendency to be professional, to play the expected role.

In order to see and hear and not merely participate, there must be a mental stepping backward for an interval of semidetached observation. Only so is it possible to capture sufficient details to create emotions instead of talking about them.

4. *Create situations listeners can enter.*

Concrete descriptive details combine to form situations that invite participation. Vague references bid only for spectators at a distance.

If I were to talk at length about my having been deeply moved by watching the setting of my son's broken arm, this would constitute a report of my feelings. But when I describe some factors that contributed to my mood, you are brought into the experience and feel with me. To re-create a moving situation is quite different from testifying to having been deeply moved.

Words that name colors, shapes, sounds, odors, and other tangibles help create backgrounds that evoke moods. Anything that moves you can move your listeners—provided they are brought into firsthand encounter with stimuli that produced the emotion.

It is one thing to become eloquent about the way religious faith adds to the joy of aged and lonely folk. It is quite a different thing to depict an incident so that listeners participate in it and draw their own conclusions.

During a preaching mission in a western city, the visiting minister was struck by the fact that one old woman always sat on the front pew. He fell into conversation with her and learned she would be eighty-six on her next birthday. A widow for nineteen years, she walked three blocks each way twice daily for the services of the week.

When her husband died, she had to pay nine hospital bills and the undertaker. "It took about all we had," she confessed. So her support was reduced to $54.30 a month. Each month, $50 went toward the cost of room and board in the rest home where she lived largely at the expense of her sons. "With that $50 gone, it leaves me $4.30 for spending and giving," she said.

"The loneliness has been the worst part. My boys are far away. All my friends are dead. If it wasn't for the church, I don't think I could live. One night, lying in bed, the Lord sent an old tune into my head. I hadn't heard it in years, till he put it there. Since then, I've sung it whenever the going gets hard."

She tossed her white locks; eighty-five-year-old eyes sparkling, she lifted her cracked voice in grateful praise, "Never alone; no, never alone!"

Because emotion-charged stories have such dynamic, there are dangers associated with use of them. So it is necessary to adopt a personal code of ethics. No precise rules can be offered; every man must devise his own set of standards. Yet some warnings are in order.

Guard against using emotion for its own sake. It is easy to develop skill in techniques, and then to use them with little regard for ends to which they are subordinate.

Respect the privacy of those with whom you deal. Incidents from the parish are likely to be identified even when names are withheld. There are enough vivid insights available outside your contacts with present parishioners to yield more material than you can use. In reporting experiences involving persons outside your parish, it is wise to alter details enough to prevent identification.

Avoid displaying your own emotions in order to win approval or admiration. Because religion is vital only when emotional currents run deep, it is easy to exploit this factor and turn the pulpit into a show place.

At the rodeo, riders mount bucking broncos and wait in the chutes for their turn before the crowd. Attendants often slap a horse's face, twist his tail, and at the crucial moment touch him with an electric shock stick. A veteran mount in whom frenzy has been invoked may buck elaborately until the whistle blows, then trot sedately to the corral. Such ersatz ecstasy may be suitable for the rodeo, but not for the house of the Lord.

Do not refuse to employ the powerful effects of emotion, but take care that you observe and sometimes revise your personal code of ethics.

11
Thank God for
Our Troubles!

FROM BIRTH TO DEATH, WE ARE REQUIRED TO MAKE OUR WAY around and over obstacles. One of Dickens' characters said we are "pitched neck and crop into the world, to play at leap-frog with its troubles." [1]

Problems and difficulties may be regarded as negative forces that threaten to reduce the meaning of life. Or they may be seen as positive ones that can increase life's significance.

Viewed in the latter fashion, trouble is among the most pervasive of factors that can contribute to tuning your ears and sharpening your eyes. By sustaining a life context that includes problems, God gives us opportunities for deliverance. At the same time, he "openeth their ears in oppression" (Job 36:15). Provided we use our difficulties as hearing aids, in time of stress we will catch life-transforming whispers.

It was not until he had wrestled all night that Jacob was given the blessing that transformed him into Israel. During a time of trouble so acute that he could not speak coherently, one ancient seeker came to see that his inability to sleep was because "thou holdest mine eyes waking" (Ps. 77:4). That is, God is a dynamic participant in every state of wretchedness. He holds our eyes open so that we may see fresh truth through the spectacles of trouble.

To recognize this is to acquire a new and revealing viewpoint. Such an outlook shapes and conditions the situation man-plus-trouble. It gives positive rather than negative direction to weary, burdened seeking. Not so much "even in trouble" as "especially in trouble," the ardent seeker for messages from the Father will succeed in finding them. At least four major sets of effects make periods of struggle especially fruitful.

1. *Concern serves to focus your perception.*

As a receiving set for signals, you are far more complex and sensitive than any equipment built for use in radio, TV, radar, or photography. You are under ceaseless bombardment by stimuli that range from light waves to mechanical vibrations.

Numerous thinkers, including Bergson, have argued that a major role of the brain and nervous system is to eliminate—tune out—the majority of signals received in any situation. If you tried to notice all stimuli of any moment, you would be overwhelmed with insignificant factors. So your brain screens out most signals and permits you to give attention to a few significant ones.

"Significance" of those things we see and hear and feel is not a constant factor, but a variable. Problems of the moment are major factors that affect my judgment of what is important to me. Consequently, those issues with which I now wrestle function somewhat like magnets with positive and negative poles. Each problem that holds my attention attracts a few signals and repels many others.

Absorbed by an urgent telephone call made from a booth in a strange city, it is easy to overlook bold instructions. Many a caller, temporarily blinded by eagerness to reach his party, has dropped in a dime without noticing directions to dial before paying. Yet it was a gripping personal problem that helped make Alexander Graham Bell sensitive to clues other men overlooked. He was so eager to find a way to improve the hearing of his sweetheart that he found and organized principles that led to invention of the telephone.

In somewhat the same way, the blindness of Louis Braille led him to focus on how the sightless may communicate with one another. One biographer says the story of his life can be put into one sentence: "Total blindness did not overcome him; it gave him new problems." [2] His area of interest being brought into sharp focus, Braille discovered a new world at his fingertips.

2. *Trouble is the great awakener.*

Any context in which you can be thoroughly comfortable is likely to prove deadening. A seed wrapped in sterilized cotton and sheltered in a vault may lie there a long time, but it will not sprout. Another seed, tossed where it will be chilled by winter before being warmed and wet by spring rains, will be awakened and will yield fruit. For it has had to die in order to live.

So it is with our souls. Immanuel Kant suggested that lacking the stimulus of problems, early man might have lived so blissfully that he would have been little better than the sheep he tended. "Man wishes harmony," he said; "but Nature knows better what is good for such as he; she will have discord." [3]

At a state fair a few years ago, one of the most interesting exhibits was in the reptile house. A skeptic might have had doubts about the shrunken head from South America. It looked like vulcanized rubber from Dayton, Ohio. But the coral snake was genuine, for it was wriggling. And the mynah bird had a rich vocabulary.

After inspecting two iguanas, I paused with my younger son to see the prize of the show, three pythons from India. Two of them were full grown. The attendant told us with pride that the larger one was forty feet long and weighed three hundred pounds, while his companion weighed just twenty pounds less.

"Do you mean to tell us," I said with some indignation, "that you've taken our money to let us stand here with only a sheet of glass between us and those monsters?"

He looked me up and down and laughed knowingly. "You don't have anything to be afraid of, mister. See how they're curled up with their heads in the middle? They're harmless as puppies. We keep their stomachs full of hamburger and we have the thermostat set where they can sleep all the time they're not eating!"

How many persons do you know who think they'd like to live like that? A stomach full of hamburger, and the thermostat set just right to sleep—the great American dream at the midpoint of the twentieth century!

God didn't intend for those whom he visits to live like that. So God wove troubles and problems and struggles into the context of his universe. Socially as well as individually, tragedy may be the most potent of all awakening forces. To be at ease in Zion is to be in a comfortable state marked by absence of sharp-edged questions and by lethargy in seeking answers.

Wrestling with a problem creates imbalance and dissatisfaction. In a state of tension, we may ask questions that never before occurred to us. We may come to fresh recognition of our own inadequacy—a necessary prerequisite to acceptance of divine aid. That is why Paul insisted that he gloried "in infirmities, in reproaches, in necessities, in persecutions, in distresses" (II Cor. 12:10).

Such a state is very far from that of wallowing in self-pity and exhibition of wounds. It has nothing in common with the attitude of whining and appealing for sympathy.

For this is the key to absolute victory! To regard your problems as heaven-sent gifts is to look at each with eyes that see. Though never to be sought for its own sake, trouble becomes a blessing. It opens eyes, reveals new truths, serves as a goad to drive the pilgrim forward toward the City of God.

Every difficulty and vexation is met with a bold query: "What does this say to me? What new truth about God does it convey? How can it sharpen my vision and tune my ears so I can receive messages I have always been too dull to catch?"

3. *Difficulties give energy for effort.*

One of Paul's most sublime letters was written out of his concern lest the "speaking with tongues" get out of control in the church at Corinth. Lacking the stimulus of major problems in one of his congregations, he would have had no incentive to analyze the nature of spiritual gifts.

In his hour of climactic challenge even the Saviour was tempted to seek relief from torment. He rejected the idea of being saved from the cross and found power to walk toward it by recognizing that "for this cause came I unto this hour" (John 12:27).

Trouble can be compared with a coiled steel spring. It sinks under weight only to throw one high in the air when it recoils. He who deliberately uses such a situation is like an athlete on

102

a trampoline. By co-operating with the "down-up" cycle, you can bounce higher than you can jump!

Any situation lacking the capacity to injure may be without potential for inducing growth.

One March afternoon I saw the sun and clouds staging a breath-taking display. Thin dark clouds were spread across the sky in layers of varying density. As the sun sank beneath the uppermost layer, glowing ruby in its visible portions, it seemed to be dipping into a colossal sea. Minutes later only the top segment of the orb was visible; from this crown of glory, it shed a ladder-like path of crimson upward. Then the sun disappeared completely, only to emerge once more, bottom-first. For seventeen minutes it continued an ever-changing exhibition of matchless beauty.

Had the sun been bright enough to hurt my eyes, it might have warmed snow-flecked fields. Subdued so that it was beautiful but not hurtful, it lacked the power to stimulate growth of plants. Henry Suso declared that "suffering is the ancient law of love; there is no quest without pain, there is no lover who is not also a martyr." [4]

4. *New meanings emerge under the impact of problem.*

In ordinary situations, we do not recognize the grandeur of that system of muscles which keep our heads erect. In order to reveal their manifold functions and the glory of the Creator who shaped them, neck muscles must become temporarily stiff. Then they witness eloquently in every activity from climbing out of bed to parking a car.

By having a stiff neck for three days, you may be ushered into fresh understanding of the Father's marvelous provision.

Any difficulty can reveal factors and forces you would not otherwise perceive.

On a typical January afternoon, the sky may be so hazy that it is hard to see where clouds begin and it is impossible to notice raindrops in the air. Yet the reality of their fall is clear from the way they spatter when they hit. Plunging drops suddenly become visible when they meet obstacles.

Israelites were at first baffled when confronted by the obstacle of preserving their worship patterns in captivity. Yearning for Zion but forced to dwell in Babylon, they lifted their voices in a plaintive query: "How shall we sing the Lord's song in a strange land?" (Ps. 137:4).

With minor variations, this note runs through all experience. It is especially loud in captivity, but it may be sounded during a move that involves going no farther than across town. It applies to every situation of change—taking a new job, affiliating with a different church, facing the emptiness that results from death of a loved one.

As the children of Israel gradually came to recognize, the truth is that we cannot sing precisely the same old song in the new context. Because of the stress, the song will either be worse or better. New depth came to Israel's knowledge of God during the Babylonian captivity. Each period of struggle can be creative.

"Bless them which persecute you: bless, and curse not" (Rom. 12:14). Surface views to the contrary, this is not an exhortation to apathy—not from Paul of Tarsus! Instead of being a passive way of escape, it is a positive formula.

Make every problem a goad, pricking you into new encounter with God. Deliberately examine each trouble, turning it about until you find a facet that serves to reflect divine light. Refuse to accept any persecution—whether by men or events—as meaningless. Seize hold of each and wrestle with it; for divine things may come as truly of wrestling with problems as of wrestling with angels. That is the essence of Miguel de Unamuno's prayer: "May God deny you peace, but give you glory." [5]

12

Methods to Make Problems
Yield Fruit

THROUGHOUT THIS BOOK, WE HAVE SEEN THAT POSSIBILITIES OF dialogue are without limit. Any event or situation can be a messenger from God. John even depicts six-winged beasts full of eyes as being engaged in ceaseless praise (Rev. 4:8). Perhaps that is his way of saying that even the most frightful of creatures may serve as signs pointing to God.

Every event and every creature sing the praises of the Creator who is above and beyond the time and space in which men frame theories and form philosophies. Nothing is without capacity to sing hymns to Jehovah, provided men with ears stand by to listen. Every tragedy and monstrosity bear a message from on high, but only those who seek such messages will receive them. Others will turn away in perplexity, having seen nothing but the grotesque and having heard no note of praise.

Some specific practices will help you to tune your ears for keener hearing through problems.

1. *Cultivate a sense of wonder.*

Possession of eyes does not guarantee discovery of marvels. Eyes of an ostrich often weigh twice as much as its brain.

Reverent wonder serves as a magnifying glass to reveal meanings invisible to the naked eye of complacency. In a monumental

106

study of medieval life, Huizinga suggests that whole cultures so centered upon knowing the Saviour that revelation came from the most remote sources. "A poor nun carrying wood to the kitchen imagines she carries the cross; a blind woman doing the washing takes the tub for the manger and the washhouse for the stable." [1]

Pause before denouncing such an insight as strained to the point of delusion. Schweitzer's three word formula that transformed his life—"Reverence for Life"—came to him while sitting on the deck of a little African steamer with hippopotamuses all about.[2]

He who succeeds in discovering the divine in every hour will abandon all entertaiment as dull by comparison. God's only category of action is that of the wonderful. He does nothing that is dull or prosaic; his every act is exalted and mysterious. A single stalk of bitterweed or a bleaching sand dollar points to marvels beyond human imagination.

"Cursed be the dullard who destroys wonder!" cries Alfred North Whitehead.[3] This is simply another way of phrasing the formula of Dr. Johnson, "we cease to wonder at what we understand." [4]

Accept such a philosophy and every item of experience becomes a source of praise. Flowing poetry of a diamondback rattler crawling from a shrub is a witness to the Creator whose works make all the hinges and joints designed by men seem clumsy. One seed pod from a cottonweed exhibits engineered packaging so complex that no factory on earth would attempt to match it.

On the morning after an October funeral, friends visited the cemetery to see the flowers. They suddenly realized that bees were working in blossoms that marked the resting place of a body that had ceased to function. Yellows, reds, and lavenders of funeral sprays had signaled God's wee creatures to come gather the final bits of nectar for perpetuation of life in the hive during the winter ahead. In the midst of death, we are face to face with life.

There are marvels and glories everywhere to be had for the seeing. "O wonderful, wonderful, and most wonderful wonderful! and yet again wonderful!" exults Shakespeare.

Part of the glory of a man who succeeds in communicating with others—whether he be playwright or preacher—lies in his capacity to discover stupendous things in the everyday. Augustine became absorbed with wonder at the power of memory, suddenly recognized that man himself is marvelous beyond understanding. "Yet, men go to admire the mountains' peaks, giant waves in the sea, the broad courses of rivers, the vast sweep of the ocean, and the circuits of the stars—and they leave themselves behind!" [5]

That was not the case with those who reported deeds and sayings of the Word made flesh. Disciples had already participated in many marvels, but when their Master raised up a girl of twelve, "immediately they were overcome with amazement" (Mark 5:42 R.S.V.).

Gospel writers see no limit to the capacity for wonder. There is no indication that they feel readers may become surfeited with marvels and begin to take them for granted. Instead, the evangelists tell us that every fresh meeting with the Saviour can be an occasion for astonishment.

Capacity for wonder grows, rather than shrinks, with use. A man who finds it hard to wonder at anything will shrug aside a

108

mighty miracle. A man who has cultivated wonder at the work of the Creator can see a miracle in any event.

If ten men have been healed of leprosy, a situation is created in which it is easy to regard the cure as established and to shrug off the eleventh healing as commonplace. But according to the viewpoint of gospel writers, the eleventh cure is no less remarkable, no less earth-shaking, no less a source of marvel and praise than the first.

Much of our thin, empty living results from the inability to treat the billionth occurrence of a miracle as being equal in rank with the first.

2. *Attack several problems at once.*

An established interest serves as a magnet to attract clues. Hence persons who are looking for evidence are likely to find it.

A sermon subject selected well in advance of the time it will be used functions in this way. By keeping several in mind, you do not have to use time and energy in frantic searching for illustrative materials. You stumble on them in the course of other activities. Because your mind is poised, events and experiences that relate to your current list of subjects are magnified. They almost seem to force themselves upon the consciousness and insist upon being recognized.

When you lack mental focus, your day may prove empty of insight. Unless your mind is alert, you may rush past a suggestive situation so rapidly you do not see its message.

Travelers on the highways react the same way. That is why it is necessary to erect signs such as "Picnic Table Ahead." Unless expectantly alert, even those who want to eat by the roadside will speed past picnic spots. Persons who failed to pack a lunch will not be halted even when advance notice has prepared them to see empty tables.

This factor raises questions about erection of roadside signs by religious groups. One of the most common proclaims simply that "CHRIST IS THE ANSWER." Such signs are erected in good faith, but overlook a major aspect of discovery.

Until you are confronted with a definite problem, its answer has no significance for you. There is no point of contact. For you, the answer is not so much false as it is meaningless. In order to seize on it as meaningful, you must come to grips' with a problem in such fashion that you end with a jigsaw puzzle from which some key pieces are missing. Then, and only then, does the answer become relevant and dynamic—an organizing center about which to arrange other pieces of evidence.

Given clear orientation toward half a dozen scripture passages or topics or Christian doctrines, you are alert for "answers." Things seen are meaningful, because they fit into the puzzles on which you are currently working.

Some men like to use index cards on which sermon topics for the immediate future are listed; others prefer to rely on their memory. Whatever the mechanical process that suits your personality, the important factor is eagerness to recognize pertinent material when it is met. No other single practice requires so little effort or yields such rich fruit as that of selecting topics in advance and finding material almost as though by accident.

3. *Help men value God's gift of struggle.*

Hosts of persons yearn for peace of mind. It is natural to turn toward religion as a major pathway to this goal; hence many people in our time regard the spiritual quest as a way to ease and plenty.

Here is a great opportunity for those of us who stand behind the pulpit: to lift up a better way, by stressing the growth-inducing role of struggle. Let us not only give thanks to God that he has placed us as witnesses within a context of tension; let us also lead men to praise him for this creative quality of our universe.

Men and women are like carbonated beverages bottled under pressure. Take off the cap, ease the pressure, and in twenty-four hours we lose all our fizz.

Ortega y Gasset holds that the creative potential of Goethe was partly dissipated by the fact that he had the misfortune to win fame very early. As a result, "Goethe became accustomed to floating on life—he forgot that he was shipwrecked. Many of the activities that were destiny in him degenerated into hobbies." [6]

Let us help men to thank God for the opportunity to make creative response to life's crushing blows. It is the heavy feet of oxen that serve to tread out the corn, separating precious grain from its concealing and confining husk.

At the end of a corridor in an aluminum and plate glass office building, there is an "EXIT" sign. Painted on rippled glass, the notice is illuminated day and night. In all structures of any size that man builds, persons who come in are concerned to know the way out. We do not want to get into anything that requires such loyalty and dedication that there is no exit.

So long as there remains a way to get out—an exit—the soul is safe; it can preserve its independence. Only when we embrace a course that has no turning, enter a house that has no exit, are we wholly committed.

Conscious entrance into the state of grateful response to

problems is one way of making such commitment. This is the road of fear and trembling—and victory.

At Ephesus, Paul rejoiced that "a great door and effectual is opened unto me, and there are many adversaries" (I Cor. 16: 9). Such a combination of factors is not accidental, but inevitable. Every great opportunity involves difficulties; conditions conducive to struggle are basic to openings.

To seek opportunity without adversaries is to search for coins that have been split in two and have no value except for their metal. Conversely, to come upon a half-buried problem is to discover a rich set of opportunities if it is turned over and viewed from the other side. So regarded, first fruits of the spiritual quest are not to be gathered in a state of peace. Rather, they are to be gained by creative response to challenges.

One morning in autumn, a visitor on the campus of a western college went to the administration building to mail a letter. Just one person was ahead of him, a woman of thirty, standing quietly on the third step of a double flight of stairs leading to the second floor. His "hello" brought a quick smile and response from her.

After dropping his letter in the chute, he pushed through swinging glass doors and turned back to watch.

She was still standing on the step reached before he entered. After a long pause, she lifted her left leg to the step above. Pushing with one crutch under a humped right shoulder, and almost clawing with the other crutch, she swung her inert right leg up one step. In a burst of striving, she climbed four steps before pausing for another long rest. She had started to class at 7:20 A.M., but she would be there for the ringing of the bell.

As much as any other message, the churchgoer needs to hear

over and over that in climbing the stairs of life it isn't the number of steps one negotiates in a bound, but the pressing forward that defines success.

4. *Encourage men to center on major issues.*

God has so fashioned us that we cannot avoid using intellectual and spiritual muscles. We engage in some kind of struggle, on some level, during most of our waking moments. So the choice is not whether to wrestle with problems, but what kind of problems will engage us.

Arnold Bennett urged that we select major issues and strive to master them as an antidote to worry. For he held that worry is a distortion or misuse of creative capacity. Jesus warned his hearers to take stock of themselves "lest at any time your hearts be overcharged with surfeiting, and drunkenness, and cares of this life" (Luke 21:34).

At first look, this seems a strange trinity. We are prone to feel that dissipation and drunkenness are much worse than mere worry. But in some respects, worry is as damaging as drunkenness; both engage attention and inhibit sensitivity. One can become so absorbed with a trifle that he has no time or energy for a supreme issue.

Even the minister faces a major challenge here. It is easy to let the business of the kingdom degenerate into busyness.

We tend to center on petty affairs, magnifying them until they dominate consciousness, because preoccupation with them makes us insensitive to grand issues of life and death, time and eternity, good and evil.

Absorption with surface issues to the exclusion of fundamental ones tends to produce persons like the man Chesterton described as knowing the last word about everything and the first word about nothing.

There are intriguing questions concerning the contemporary passion for western stories on TV as well as for detective yarns and comic strips. By giving attention to fictional characters who tie all their problems in neat bundles, we shift attention from riddles of existence that would baffle us if we let them emerge into consciousness. Much of modern civilization is aimed at making it easy for us not to think. We pay anything to be entertained—by someone else's efforts; and we waste more time and effort avoiding mental work than we would use actually thinking.

Obtaining food is simple for the modern westerner, and he has few opportunities to pit himself against forces of nature. So the executive is prone to exert his energy by trying to defeat business competitors or by winning the golf trophy at the country club.

Such majoring on minors need not prevail. Through witness of ministers dedicated to searching for late word from Jehovah, men can be challenged to center on significant issues.

Karl Jaspers defines man as "that creature which poses problems beyond his powers." [7] Cosmic riddles abound—issues big enough to merit the best efforts we can exert.

Informed that members of his family were seeking him, Jesus tossed out a question too profound for an answer: "Who is my mother, or my brethren?" (Mark 3:33). For the Master every event was the springboard for a profound riddle. He took no ideas for granted, but jolted minds by turning light on some neglected facet of the universally accepted. For him everything had religious implications and was related to all-absorbing issues of life and death.

To ask a new question about the obvious is more difficult than to travel abroad or inquire along fringes of knowledge. "For us," points out Schweitzer, "the great men are not those who solved the problems, but those who discovered them." [8] By example as well as exhortation, we can inspire men to abandon worry and busyness in favor of absorption with significant issues.

5. *Capitalize on the dynamic of discovery.*

A sermon born of personal striving for solutions is likely to be expressed with vigor. He who has made a discovery gains not only something to say, but also power with which to say it. Simply to be confronted with a situation where speech is expected—whether from the pulpit or elsewhere—is no guarantee that communication will take place.

Spontaneous praise of God, as opposed to lifeless participation in conventional acts and words, must always be fresh. Praise keeps no better than manna. It grows out of a vivid instance of participation in the ongoing drama of creation. This constitutes entrance into a larger room. It is the source of much joy linked with invention and artistic creativity as well as worship. It confers intangible but real power in making public what has been discovered.

That is to say, in order to stir men into creative encounter with God, you must yourself be continually aglow with the thrill of discovery. Horace said of the would-be persuader: "If you want me to weep, you must first grieve yourself." A glimpse of the divine, whether in the handshake of a dying saint, or in the matchless symmetry of a hen's egg, thrills and fills. It leaves one's clothes smelling of myrrh and cassia, and the soul positively aglow.

Much of the rapture of such a moment is linked with having come into larger understanding. The seeker has found what for him in that moment is new. He is an ingredient in the creative union. He has given and received in the alchemy of knowing—so dynamic that the nearest analogy is that of intoxication. Hence he gains power to transmit his message. In a sense he is secondary and his message is primary.

When a sensitive and gifted man conducts a symphony, the music flows through him. He becomes an instrument for the melody. Shoulders, neck, head, hips, legs, face, arms, and hands are channels for the flow of melodic meaning. In limited fashion, music is incarnate—made flesh—so that every quivering muscle is subordinate to the music that holds the man captive.

Because Jesus always taught with authority, "the people were astonished at his doctrine" (Matt. 7:28). They sat up and listened even when they were not stirred to believe. Whether they wished to do so or not, they could not ignore the power of messages still glowing from the fires of moving toward the Father for fresh answers.

There is no vitality in preaching which lacks a degree of astonishment. We may be past masters in the art of going through the ritual—verbal and physical—yet blind to the way our confrontation of listeners can bring about a state of astonishment.

Preaching, so-called, that is dull and listless and lacking in the creative spark is not really preaching. "Conditioning" would be a better label for it; there is no eager leap on the part of listeners. Such response comes only when there is vigorous witness to truth recently and personally discovered.

116

Go to the pastures and fields, and be wise. Recognize that the fruitless one who refrains from the trauma of cultivation and from the pangs of birth, who prefers to lie fallow, bypasses the unutterable joy of joining in the symphony of universal praise to the Creator who wove creative capacity into his own.

13
Think Yourself Out of
Your Own Skin

AT A "POP" CONCERT, A HANDSOME TENOR SANG THE "SERENADE"
from Romberg's *The Student Prince.* One listener leaned forward with a beneficent smile on her face. Her lips and throat
began to pulsate as the vigorous young blond raised his powerful voice in "Love me, or I die!" Oblivious to the masses about
her, the total engrossment of this listener made it clear that
for her the fervent song was directed especially to the little gray-
haired woman in Section L.

Though I was seated only a few feet away and was exposed
to the same influences, I did not hear as she did. Really to thrill
to such a serenade, I should have to enter her mood and listen
to the vibrant words as addressed to me by my lover.

Here is a major clue to ways the seeker for insight can multiply
the number and extend the scope of his discoveries. To the
degree that I succeed clumsily and briefly in listening through
ears of others, temporarily ceasing to hear through the receiving
set that is my own personality, I shall be showered with fresh
melodies.

Part of the dynamic of Paul's letters stems from the fact that
it was in the mood of sharing his own outlook that he urged

those who would be transformed to "rejoice with them that do rejoice, and weep with them that weep." (Rom. 12:15).

My private world is very small. It lacks many features that contribute to the richness of your world. Before I can enter yours, I must either duplicate your experiences or participate vicariously in them through sympathetic striving to look through your eyes.

Balzac said of the strangers among whom he was thrown: "I was able to wed myself to their life; I felt their rags on my back; I walked with my feet in their torn shoes." Small wonder, then, that he could conclude that "their desires, their needs, everything passed into my soul, and my soul passed into their's." [1]

For maximum fruitfulness, such meetings must be specific rather than general. They must be entered in definite situations. Some ways to participate in them are suggested below.

1. *Strive for the viewpoint of a child.*

Childlikeness is a major asset to the seeker for God. Part of the reason lies in the fact that a child is open and receptive. His world is more fluid than that of an adult. Some of the rigid outlines of the adult world are plastic when viewed through the eyes of a child or a poet.

In a British film version of *Tales of Hoffmann* some of the most vivid scenes are linked with the second tale. In it, the cosmopolitan Hoffmann falls in love with a dark-haired beauty who tempts him and then leaves him—having sold herself to a magician for a promise of jewelry.

At one point the magician snatches bits of molten wax from red, white, and green candles. Under his touch they are transformed to rubies, diamonds, and emeralds. Once, after the girl has put these gems around her neck, the stones are briefly turned back into daubs of wax.

It is the very highest kind of magic to be able to see gems in bits of wax. An equally keen, but quite different, eye is required to see bits of wax in the stones of an expensive necklace. Children are generally more adept than are adults in fostering such transformations.

So it is rare for a man or woman to succeed in viewing any situation through eyes of a preschool child. By deliberate striving, it can sometimes be done in limited fashion.

One hot, cloudy morning I slipped into the fourth chair at a barber shop. My neighbor in the fifth chair, a blonde of two, was having a dreadful time getting her bangs trimmed.

A casual glance raised questions about the wailing. For the girl's mother stood by the chair and brushed to prevent hair from getting into her eyes. There was nothing ferocious about the barber; he was grandfatherly and solicitous. Still his young customer kicked and blubbered.

Clumsily I tried to think myself out of my own skin and into the skin of the child. Though I had only limited success, the process led to the quick transformation of my point of view.

Suddenly I was no longer slouched comfortably in an overstuffed chair just right for a man of my size. Instead, I found myself perched precariously on a board placed across the arms of a steel and leather monster. With my legs swinging so that I could barely touch bottom, I was surrounded by bright lights and strange noises. Pungent odors from hair tonic and shoe polish assailed my nostrils. A huge stranger in a white coat was standing over me. Scissors in hand, he darted them at my head: "Snip, snip, snip."

It was here that I lost the viewpoint of the child and returned to my own identity, for my moment of insight was interrupted by the fact that I found myself about to cry!

To the degree that you survey a familiar situation through eyes of a child, you will discover new and exotic elements. In his lectures on Shakespeare, Coleridge suggested that such insights are gained from the perspective of "a soul unsubdued by habit, unshackled by custom." [2]

An early president of Columbia College, author of a Hebrew dictionary and authority on many erudite subjects, succeeded, in a time of family stress, in slipping into the mood of a child. Emerging from it with vivid new impressions, Clement C. Moore wrote "The Night Before Christmas."

To the degree that you succeed in enlarging your world by looking through eyes of boys and girls, you will enhance your capacity for insight.

2. *Seek for the outlook of the novice.*

Scripture repeatedly warns against complacency and assurance. Persons who are least receptive to divine messages are those revered as experts. Lawyers, Pharisees, and learned interpreters of Moses have ears that are closed to the call of the Messiah.

Every beginner is acutely conscious of his status. He knows that he does not know. He looks at every set of practices with an untaught eye and wonders: "What does it mean? Why is it done this way?"

In contrast, the expert knows why it is done and what it means. He inhibits discovery by his mastery of conventional understanding. This is part of the "hardening" of the Hebrews. It is the basis for the fact that "knowledge puffeth up" (I Cor.

8:1). One who knows the answers, and knows that he knows them, loses capacity to see new things.

Such a person is like the blind man described by Augustine. He stands in the sun, but his eyes are incapable of being affected. So while the sun is present to him, he is absent from the sun.

Familiarity, competence, and confidence serve as screens to filter out many wave lengths. Hence a situation or object may be so dimly lighted that it looks quite dull.

Take for example the dashboard of an automobile. No matter what decorative changes may be made in new models, the general appearance is standard: controls for heater, radio, windshield wiper, and lights—plus a speed indicator with numbers to about 120. You and I glance casually at such an array and find nothing exciting.

Great-grandpa would be incapable of seeing through the eyes of a veteran driver who has been behind the wheel for 150,000 miles. His lack of familiarity would require him to examine things from the viewpoint of a novice. His dashboard served to shelter him from mud and water kicked up by Old Sam. So even if he happened to notice them, he wouldn't have any idea that the numbers on the dashboard of a car refer to miles per hour.

Once this matter was pointed out to him, he would marvel at the way such speeds are attained through union of oxygen with fractions of petroleum whose origin, millions of years ago, was a result of activity by sea animals and plants extinct before man appeared on earth. With his naïve views on automobiles and petroleum and his sensitivity to the message of Genesis, great-grandpa might find stupendous signs of the Creator's work in the numerals that adorn the dashboard of a car.

3. *Adopt the viewpoint of one who offends.*

It is comparatively easy to achieve a friend's frame of reference. It is harder, and more rewarding, to attempt a brief peek
through eyes of an opponent or one who repels. Even a brief
encounter with such a person—a tentative meeting through the
magic of words—can be revealing.

A rider entering a coach on an early morning train, fumbled
as he attempted to take out cash to pay his fare. Punch in hand,
the Irish conductor stuck out his bulldog chin and snapped:
"Well, are you gonna keep me standing here an hour?"

His passenger's mouth dropped open at such a reaction to a
five-second delay. For a moment he debated asking the conductor
about the effects of his manner upon the public relations program of his railroad. Having reluctantly discarded this course,
he waited until the train was under way and struck up a conversation.

Before three sentences had been exchanged, it developed that
foot trouble bothered the conductor so much he had to go to
the doctor twice a week. He had to lose twenty pounds before
Christmas. On this particular day he was on a special run that
came only once every six weeks. Instead of returning home, he
had to spend the week end in a hotel. He had twenty-one cars
to tend, and a passenger in a wheel chair seemed likely to miss her
connection.

Knowing all this the rider ceased to be offended by his grumpi-
ness. Failure to buy a ticket in advance suddenly took on new
importance. The passenger looked at himself through the blood-
shot eyes of the old conductor and saw a stranger who didn't
bother to help a fellow keep his paperwork to a minimum.

Almost as in a flood there came recognition that in any situation where I am conscious of being offended, a different perspective may put me in the spotlight as an offender.

Tolerance and self-criticism are not the only fruits of assuming the viewpoint of one who seems to deserve condemnation. Any sympathetic journey of exploration may heighten awareness.

New understanding of man's inhumanity to man came to a college dean as a result of a single glance through the eyes of a student in trouble. Dick faced dismissal because of a drinking bout. So he took his punishment calmly and asked no favors. They talked for half an hour and Dick explained that his father had worked in a distillery until his death. At seven, the orphan began work as a shoeshine boy in taverns of a polyglot steel town.

As an aside, he recalled that there were fifteen taverns on the main street, and each was a port of entry for a house of prostitution. "When I first started shining," he recalled, "I thought it was impossible that any women in the world could be as beautiful as those women."

What a stupendous feat it would be, if God-fearing church folk could see—really see—the poor painted ones of their town as beautiful in the eyes of their Maker. So beautiful that there would be no more exploitation of slum property by pew holders; so beautiful that there would be no condemnation, but only redeeming love.

4. *See from the perspective of various backgrounds.*

Continually to look through the eyes of a minister, who is a person of prestige, is to overlook many opportunities for enlargement.

One morning a minister stopped at a small cafeteria for lunch.

124

He ate with little appetite, for he was chafing at having been refused honorary membership in the country club. Obviously, people did not appreciate him as they should—and besides, he would have to continue paying greens fees.

Walking back to his car, which he ruefully reflected was already a year old, his eye was caught by a beggar. This fellow was a real physical wreck. His right arm was off at the elbow; his right foot was twisted ninety degrees from normal and sheathed in three or four layers of automobile casing. His right eye was grotesquely out of line, and his left leg—apparently off somewhere near the knee—terminated in a homemade peg leg tipped with metal.

An introductory question suggested that he must have been in a bad wreck. "No, sir," the beggar explained, "I was partly born this way. Then I got blood poisoning and lost this arm. But I didn't quit work till a year ago. Yessir, started when I was eight, and I'm sixty-eight now."

"Now that you've had to go to begging, how do you get back and forth?"

"I ride the bus. Crawl up the steps, real good. I can climb a ladder right now."

He said he collected enough to pay his room rent and buy food. "I ain't never been behind with my room rent. Been stayin' with the same folks nineteen years. They let me sleep in the mornings."

There came that significant lull that indicates either the end of a conversation or the most significant moment in it. Peering up through those twisted eyes, gesturing with his poor stump of an arm, the wretch surveyed his new friend. "Don't never give up, mister," he urged. *"Don't never give up!"*

In different but equally vivid fashion, an attendant at a zoo gave fresh perspective. Visiting the zoo on a gray afternoon in March, we found it all but deserted. So at the cage of a little owl-faced monkey, it was easy to open a conversation with the keeper.

I inquired how they select the diet for such animals; the keeper answered in one sentence and asked eight-year-old Bill how he'd like to have a banana. Questioned about the growling of the baboon, the attendant described the animal as really dangerous, and inquired whether Bill would like to go into the cages of some harmless animals.

For its duration, our back-and-forth conversation was three-sided: with the keeper's interest centered in Bill. When we wandered on, he squatted on his heels to talk with two girls in the next party.

We came to the zoo to show Bill the animals. Their keeper, who spent eight hours a day with creatures we regarded with wonder, was hungry to enjoy banter with our children! Repeatedly, we lose capacity to see wonderful gifts of God; temporary viewing through the eyes of a stranger may afford at least a glimpse of glory.

It is easy to laugh and weep over stage plays. It is more suggestive so to share inner selves of others that we briefly become like them and weep or laugh spontaneously with them—not at them or for them. Outside the testimony of great Christian witnesses, this complex idea is best expressed by poets like Whitman:

Agonies are one of my changes of garments,
I do not ask the wounded person how he feels, I myself become the
    wounded person.[3]

5. *Explore the nonhuman world.*

Capacity to understand an ant or a violet is on an order quite different from understanding a child or an opponent. There is no way we can really enter the subhuman world. At most, we can push across some threshold for a quick glance.

Many creative souls have tried to express the importance of such intuitive crossing of boundaries. Keats declared that if a sparrow hopped about before his window, he entered its universe and with it picked in the gravel. During a gentle rain, Thoreau found himself "suddenly sensible of such sweet and beneficent society in Nature" that it seemed "every little pine needle expanded and swelled with sympathy and befriended me." [4]

Bernard Berenson traces an aesthetic awakening to a morning when he was looking at leafy scrolls on door jambs of a cathedral. "Suddenly stem, tendril, and foliage became alive," he said afterward. "I felt as one illumined, and beheld a world where every outline, every edge, and every surface was in a living relation to me and not, as hitherto, in a merely cognitive one." [5]

Wordsworth imagined himself into the heart of a daffodil, and broke into laughter. But in the primrose, he found thoughts "too deep for tears." When his imagination was keen, said Miguel de Unamuno of himself, "I feel the pain of animals, and the pain of a tree when one of its branches is being cut off." [6] Recalling a solitary walk on the first Sunday in Lent, Thomas Merton was most vividly impressed by the way "woods, hills, birds, water, and sky" spoke to him freely and intimately.[7]

6. *Fashion metaphors and epigrams.*

Once your imagination is sharpened by projection of the self into a strange context, you may succeed in discovering like factors in things considered wholly unlike. When such a common denominator has been found, it is easy to fashion a brief and pointed statement with high interest value.

Here are some examples of such epigrams:

Activism in the church is like a hen trying to lay an egg on an escalator. There's a great deal of movement, but no getting down to business.

Some sermons are like a long, pointed feather in a woman's hat. They jab menacingly in all directions, but the point's too weak to leave a mark.

Many a Sunday-school teacher is like a lightning bug. His tail light twinkles only at intervals, and he has no headlight at all. So he flies full speed in the dark.

Purple lipstick on a cigarette butt is like a mosquito bite; the sucker's gone, but she left her mark.

An example will indicate patterns of thought that are productive of such attention-getting quips.

After having finished a sandwich and coffee at a hamburger house, I decided to have pie. My waitress offered to warm my coffee; so when she handed the cup back, I poured in a new supply of cream.

Half-consciously, I noticed that the spring of the cream pitcher was defective. When I released it to close the top, milk continued to drool down the sides and drop on the counter.

This cream pitcher sits on the counter. Its one job is to give out, give out, give out. But it also has to cut off. This pitcher is like some speakers—like the man who addressed our district rally last Friday. He could give out, just like a pitcher. And he couldn't cut off any better than this one does.

That same short-order house suggests, by the way, such additional ideas as these:

Too many teachers of Sunday-school classes are like operators of third-class restaurants. They advertise country-cured ham, but actually serve warmed-over bologna.

An occasional preacher is like a bottle of red-pepper sauce. His whole life is dedicated to periodic release of a blistering torrent through a hole in his head.

7. *Extend your sensory experiences.*

In order to transform your whole system of fingertip touch experience, alter the customary length of your fingernails by a quarter of an inch. If you wish to gain new understanding of your bedroom, explore it with one shoe off and one shoe on!

In modern life, no areas of our knowing are so likely to be impoverished as those which rest on data from touch, smell, and muscles. We use our eyes and ears and tongue a great deal—clumsily, it is true—but signals from other organs of perception are likely to be ignored altogether.

We need sometimes to adopt the mood of a Halloween party. In a darkened hall of horrors, adolescent girls squeal and have a wonderful time feeling with their fingertips such things as a bowl of wet macaroni, a cold beef bone, and a dish of gelatin. When accompanied by the rattling of a chain and the odor of sprinkled tomato juice, such effects may be all but overpowering.

Our Creator has given us elaborate sets of signal-receiving equipment that we seldom use. As civilization matures, the role of the human nose becomes less and less important except as a prop for glasses. In any situation, familiar or strange, we can add to our knowledge by using organs of touch and smell and balance for reports to supplement those furnished by eyes and ears.

Experiment in capturing the essence of such experiences as: comparing the handshake of an adolescent girl, a shoeshine man, a college professor or a minister, a bell hop, and a sawmill operator; smelling an attic, a suit of clothes after three days on the train, a plowed field after a spring shower; touching chewing gum—new and used, velvet, cat's fur, screen wire; experiencing the motions of skating, bowling, dropping in an express elevator, climbing steep steps.

8. *Go outside the familiar.*

You and I tend to go through life like snails that do not move an inch without their shells. Because protective covers are sometimes shattered in time of struggle, one forced to endure the intolerable may emerge with new sensitivity. It can hardly be accidental, for example, that all these men were medical corpsmen in World War I: Ernest Hemingway, Louis Bromfield, Archibald MacLeish, Warwick Deeping, and John Dos Passos.

You do not have to drive an ambulance over battlefields in order to tighten and tune the strings on which you play for others those melodies you discover and create. Any excursion out of the ordinary, any deviation from the customary, may provide a new perspective.

One Saturday afternoon my family and I stopped for a snack after having spent three hours at the sports auditorium. We parked in our customary lot, just two blocks from a favorite eating place. Impulsively we cut through a block-long alley between two huge buildings in order to save a few steps. An hour later, returning to the car, we took the same short cut.

But darkness had fallen while we ate. We turned from a main street as bright as your living room into the sudden blackness of an alley relieved only by a faint tinge of gray at the far end. After six steps, all of us were seized with doubt. Nevertheless, we continued, and far down the tunnel caught a glimpse of a man. Too late, I remembered that I had fifty dollars in my pocket and that a few days earlier, the papers had carried the story of a clerk who was attacked for eighty cents.

Our hearts racing and our fingers stiff as we groped for one another and clutched hands, we said nothing until we found a slightly brighter alley that led off to the left. We fled gladly to the street, wonderfully and gloriously conscious of the ministry of the electric light.

Thirty seconds from every safe and familiar route, there is a strange world that includes good reasons for the heart to pound. To the degree that you deviate from the sheltered and familiar, you are likely to discover close at hand a new universe of experience.

14

New Frontiers in
Your Study

COMPARATIVELY FEW MINISTERS ACHIEVE A PATTERN OF CONTINU-
ing growth. Most of us reach a peak in mental and spiritual
achievement somewhere near middle age, then either fall back
from that level or stay on it for the rest of our lives.

No degree of enlargement through other avenues will compen-
sate for lack of intellectual growth. Pressures of the modern
parish are such that it is easy to forego any real stretching of the
mind after formal education has ceased.

Some Pitfalls to Be Avoided

Friedrich Nietzsche has a cynical beatitude which promises:
"Blessed are the sleepy, for they shall soon drop off." Three
camouflaged varieties of sleepiness are particularly likely to become pitfalls for the preacher.

1. *Satisfaction with formal education* tempts us to feel we
have all the answers we need—or have time to gain—when college and seminary are completed. Even when such a view is not
consciously held, it is easy to drift into it by default.

Every freshman is continually reminded of what he does not
know, and so is made relatively receptive to learning. He looks
at life through consciously untaught eyes. By contrast, the gradu-

ate is likely to stress his achievements. It was in the attitude of men who have just received their B.D. degrees with honors that colleagues of Nicodemus advised him to search the Scriptures in order to recognize with them that "out of Galilee ariseth no prophet" (John 7:52).

Whitehead was once asked, "At what period in your life did you begin to feel that you had a grasp of your subject?" In a fashion that an intimate friend considered somewhat brusque, the renowned philosopher gave a one-word reply:

"Never!" [1]

Every good teacher knows that formal education should be a point of departure rather than a terminus. But the schooling of a minister is unusually long and complex, sometimes fostering the illusion that one who has run to the end of that course needn't continue to strain forward. He must work and study to prepare his sermons, of course; but days of hard intellectual digging for the sake of stretching the mind are over. He has all the necessary credentials; he is educated.

Few fallacies are so pernicious—or so generally held in practice if not in theory.

2. *Pride of professional status* is among the demonic factors particularly likely to entangle the feet of a minister. By virtue of his place in the religious institution, he is a man of importance. He does not have to earn the respect of his associates; because he wears the cloth, men extend to him some of the respect they have for his office.

Corrosive effects of social status are magnified by the fact that the pulpit is among the most sheltered spots of modern society. When we stand behind it as spokesmen for the Most High, we are all but invulnerable. We continually engage in one-way

133

communication. If we say things that are wrong or silly (as any man is likely to do if he talks continuously for twenty minutes on any subject), our listeners do not challenge us. Instead, at the close of the service, they shake hands and offer congratulations on a fine message.

At a western sports show, one of the events was a log-rolling contest. Illuminated by a battery of spotlights, two big Canadians tried to spin one another from a 1600-pound peeled log. After a final ducking and round of applause, the announcer described the next act: water spaniels trained to work as retrievers.

"Watch closely, ladies and gents!" he urged. "We'll have to cut out the spotlight for this act. Dogs do not perform well under a spotlight."

Spotlights affect all on whom they shine—humans as well as canines. Because we ministers are constantly in the spotlight, we are in danger of having our vision affected without being aware of it. Our protected place of prestige fosters adoption of an easy omniscience.

Seeking an associate, a pastor applied to the placement officer of a seminary. They chatted about job requirements, and the educator inquired whether there would be regular preaching assignments. "Nope," said the minister. "No preaching for the boy. My pulpit's my throne, and I don't let anybody occupy my throne!"

Whether deliberately adopted or entered so gradually that one is not aware he holds it, such a point of view obscures vision. In many of his relationships, and especially in his role as one who habitually speaks with authority, the minister who does not consciously resist is likely to find his eyes clouded by the film of pride.

134

3. *Contentment with techniques that work* is a source of danger because it reduces incentive to achieve states that produce skills and techniques.

Describing his own homiletical methods, Paul had nothing to say about introductions and outlines. Instead, he summed up his philosophy of witness by citing David's testimony: "I believed, and therefore have I spoken" (II Cor. 4:13).

Beliefs, goals, and loyalties are prior to, and run deeper than, speech. Techniques for use of words and gestures are always secondary. To elevate a skill or method into primacy is to distort the whole role of the witness. To select some measurable "success goal" and try to use it to determine the success or failure of a sermon is to elevate the process of speaking to a position it does not deserve.

That witness who is effective must give more attention to his own knowing of God than to mechanics or results of his preaching. This is not to say that he ignores the importance of homiletical methods; on the contrary, he will do all he can to multiply avenues of expression. But he will first make sure that he continues to have fresh and valid messages to express. Otherwise he ceases to communicate and is content with going through motions.

At an industrial museum, one of the exhibits is a replica of an old-time blacksmith shop. Pumping a bellows with his left hand, the smith began heating a small iron bar. Curious spectators gathered to watch, and a child inquired what he would make. "Wait twelve minutes, and you'll see," he promised.

After four or five heatings and as many beatings, it became obvious that the bar was assuming horseshoe shape. Completed, the miniature was carefully marked at points where full-size shoes have holes for nailing to an animal's foot. "Whose horse is gonna wear it?" an onlooker demanded.

"Nobody's. They'll sell it downstairs. Next demonstration in an hour."

Sold downstairs for 25¢, his handiwork was a by-product of a demonstration. It was shaped to resemble a horseshoe, but never could be worn by a horse. Artisan though he was, the museum employee had participated in an exhibition rather than a making. His product suggested the real thing, but had no capacity to affect a life situation.

Sermons copied from messages that had dynamic in a different context are like that ersatz horseshoe. They have many characteristics of the real thing, but they cannot enter a vital relationship with life. So the most that can be said of one who excels in shaping such pieces is that he is a skilled demonstrator.

Some Approaches to Intellectual Fruitfulness

Hugh of St. Cher, a Dominican of the thirteenth century, is best known for his work in compiling the first concordance of the Scriptures. He excelled in the pulpit as well as in the study, however. His formula for effective preaching was brief: "The bow is first bent in the study, and then, in preaching, the arrow is let fly." [2]

No bending of the bow, no power for the arrow. It is that simple—and that profound. Put in the plainest possible fashion, the requirements of preaching are such that work is a basic ingredient: hard work, long work, continuous work, muscle-straining work, extensive work, intensive work. Work, work, work!

Does this seem exaggerated or pompous?

Consider that it was in the context of his interpretation of the shepherd's role that Jesus declared: "I am come that they might have life, and that they might have it more abundantly" (John 10:10). Usually treated as one of the most precious promises of the Gospel, this formula is fully as challenging as it is comforting.

Basic qualities linked with biological life are suggested in terms of intellectual and spiritual life. Only that cluster of molecules is alive which has: (a) an internal state of ordered tension; (b) a state of reciprocal tension with the environment; (c) capacity for selective interaction with external forces; and (d) capacity to reproduce itself.

That is, the state of being alive is continually uncomfortable. Dynamics of the living organism make it a system of shifting tension. There must be enlargement—fresh forays into the surroundings and new responses to signals—during every moment of life. When striving ceases, life fades and leaves behind a tensionless state we call death. Though the element of drudgery can be largely eliminated from sermon preparation, as suggested in Chapter 1, effort centered upon growth cannot.

To stave off slow death of the mind and soul, tension-inducing exercises are helpful.

1. *Embrace a program of lifelong study.*

Formality, or lack of it, is not nearly so significant as degreee of commitment to a program. It is the principle of choosing to strive, not the blueprint of a pattern of striving, that is significant. Leo Stein puts it like this: "There is self-education and education by others. There is education that is intended, and education that just happens. But of necessity there is either education or stagnation." [3]

Try an experiment. Park your car close against the curb and

parallel with it. Let it stay there until other cars have pushed close against it in front and behind. Then maneuver your car into the street.

Such a situation brings fresh appreciation of the dynamics of change. Cruising along the highway, it takes little effort to cut wheels sharply. Even with power steering, when motionless or nearly so, wheels resist so strongly that considerable pulling and grunting is required to change their course.

For dynamic in turning, there's nothing like getting in motion. Herbert Read expressed the idea more formally by saying that "in the ceaseless unfolding of existence, it is reactionary to stand still." [4]

That is, both mental and spiritual realms require continuous outreach even to maintain the *status quo*. Whether the mind is expanding or shrinking, its processes have cumulative effects. No formula deserves more profound respect than Jesus' warning-promise: "For he that hath, to him shall be given: and he that hath not, from him shall be taken away even that which he hath" (Mark 4:25).

2. *Seek enlargement as self-rewarding.*

It is not enough to embrace a program of lifelong study. Such an enterprise becomes distorted or meaningless if pursued for shallow reasons. Unless the motive is right, the activity is less than valid.

T. S. Eliot uses this paradox as the basic theme of *Murder in the Cathedral*. Faced with the prospect of martyrdom, the Archbishop of Canterbury is tempted to seek it in order to gain fame. He toys with the idea, but in a sublime moment rejects it, concluding that

138

The last temptation is the greatest treason:
To do the right deed for the wrong reason.[5]

Just as a woman may wear feathers in her hat without acquiring the power to fly, so we may spend hours with heavy books without accepting their richest gifts. To engage in a course of action for the sake of rewards external to the work performed is at best to make a living. Jesus called such a worker a hireling, and it was not a label of commendation.

Shortly after midnight a traveler stopped at a motel where a big neon sign proclaimed "Vacancy." One dim light burned outside the office, revealing the instructions, "Ring Bell."

Ringing, waiting. Ringing, waiting. While debating whether or not to leave, the prospective guest heard someone coming. Eventually the operator stumbled out barefoot in his undershirt. He nodded confirmation of the vacancy sign, handed over the key to room number twenty-two. As he opened the cash drawer, his guest noticed and commented on the stack of silver dollars it held.

No reply, not even a monosyllable. No pleasantries, no token of interest, not even a fleeting smile. He accepted the five dollars plus tax—but resented having to take it!

If I resent my work, either I am not doing the right kind of work or I have failed to find the plus-factors that can transform it. There is no significance in seeking to meditate day and night with the hope that this will bring rewards alien to the search itself. Only when fruits of searching are so prized that no other pay is needed does discipline become meaningful.

One way to foster the discovery of self-validating rewards from study is to let personal interest be a guiding factor in selecting

139

areas of inquiry and authors who deal with them. By keeping a list of "books to read," a start from any given point may lead to branching out in several directions.

Because I am deeply interested in communication, for example, I turn to *An Essay on Man*, by Ernst Cassirer. As a result of action on this established interest, there are several streams of effects.

First, I list half a dozen other volumes by Cassirer that sooner or later I want to read. Second, I find that there are intriguing factors about human communication that make the process unique; so I develop an interest in the total creative process of the creature made a little lower than the angels. This new interest leads to its own list of titles and subjects to investigate. Third, through finding that some of Cassirer's works were translated by Susanne K. Langer, I am led to discover her own *Philosophy in a New Key*. Fourth, a quick survey of literature dealing with man's sublime capacity to produce new symbols and ideas makes me acquainted with Jacques Maritain's *Creative Intuition in Art and Poetry*. Through it, I am stirred to turn to other volumes from his pen and to half a dozen works he cites.

Extending, expanding, proliferating, breeding and cross-breeding, old interests beget new ones far removed from the original. Instead of shrinking, the list expands continually. There is no prospect of ever running out of material. Life is too short to act on all the challenges spawned by a single moment of curiosity.

Pursuing such leads, staying always within the scope of some long-held or new-found interest and putting aside any volume that is dull or unduly difficult in one's present stage of understanding, the pursuit of intellectual game brings its own satisfactions. It makes no difference whether any other reward, tangible or intangible, is gained. No other is needed in order to make the quest worth while.

3. *Occasionally explore new fields.*

It is easy for us to concentrate all our time and energy within areas associated with the pulpit. It is somewhat more difficult—and wholly rewarding—to explore other areas that are challenging by virtue of their strangeness.

Moses might have missed his greatest opportunity had he not left his customary way in order to "turn aside, and see this great sight" (Exod. 3:3). God continually provides signals that can lead us to new truth. But in order to act on them, we must sometimes turn aside from habitual paths.

Modern automobiles are so built that the quickest and surest way to turn on the overhead light is to open a door. Nearly always, opening a new door of inquiry will turn on a light that floods the mind.

Many achievements of philosophy and science have been made by men who stumbled on new ideas when exploring one field from the background of competence in another. It was theological curiosity coupled with skill in logic that led Georg Cantor to blaze trails in the mathematics of infinity. William James was both a philosopher and a psychologist. Henri Bergson mastered physics before problems of time and motion led him to philosophy.

Experts of his day considered Jesus a religious heretic because he healed the sick by assuring them that their sins were forgiven. Experts of our day sometimes consider such statements to constitute medical heresy. A few pioneers are rediscovering that

141

boundaries between spiritual and physical health are not so high or so rigid as long thought.

Part of our human dilemma lies in our respect for boundaries. They are essential for thought and action, but are likely to be arbitrary. Really great innovations nearly always stem from shutting one's eyes to some set of accepted boundaries.

The creative potential of childhood is linked with the fact that youthful ones do not know enough to stay within conventional patterns. So they leap to recognition of like factors in situations we dull adults consider to be poles apart. It is disregard for boundaries that leads to some of the most delightful novelties that drop from lips of children.

In the early days of radio, a doctor's small daughter watched wide-eyed as he applied his stethoscope to a patient's chest. She stood it as long as she could, then inquired, "Get any new stations, daddy?"

Visiting an Episcopal church for the first time, a kindergarten youngster was perplexed when the choir filed in, white surplices stiff with starch. "Mama," he demanded. "Mama, are all those people going to get their hair cut?"

Ours is primarily a bacon family. But one winter evening, my wife fried link sausages. Bill, seven, was intrigued by the novel food and curious to know who would eat it. As he tried to decipher symbols printed on the sausages, they began to pop grease from the pan. "Hey, dad!" he cried. "This sausage is spitting on me!"

Such discoveries are valuable chiefly for their freshness. We laugh at them and pass them along to our friends. No matter what the degree of social significance of an insight gained from stumbling on a new relationship, for the discoverer it has dynamic because it is his. Hence in his public witnessing, such material has power that is absent from conventional and hackneyed material—no matter how significant it may be.

To multiply instances of discovery through cross-fertilization of ideas, occasionally explore new regions: biology or astronomy, history or music, art or criminology. Using interest as a criterion by which to make selections, you can't lose—and you may gain unexpected dividends!

4. *Give the classics a chance.*

Best sellers gain their places on the list partly as a result of good merchandising and partly because they have won endorsement from the viewpoint of today's cultural emphases and values.

That is a way of recognizing that a new novel or biography or volume of devotions that becomes a smash hit has been voted "superior" by jurors who represent just one cross section of mankind. A different situation prevails in the case of a book tested and approved by men of many cultural backgrounds over a period of centuries.

There are many available collections and study programs, ranging from the Harvard Classics to the Great Books Movement. None are definitive; many are suggestive. Among the most diversified and inexpensive is the paperback volume *Good Reading,* "A Guide to the World's Best Books," periodically revised and published in new editions by The New American Library.

Perhaps you are less vulnerable, but for my part, I never open a guide like that without feeling ashamed of the big gaps in my understanding. Not only have I overlooked practically all the titles that deal with major historical periods; I don't even know the names of the periods! Although I take courage from the list of standard works in anthropology and sociology, I meet my Waterloo in the economics section.

No prepared guide should be taken too seriously or followed in slavish fashion. Yet one or more will at least serve to show how vast a portion of the world's great literature has been neglected.

Of the volumes listed below, how many have you given an opportunity to fire your mind and soul? This brief list is of course suggestive, not exhaustive. It is included only to indicate that in the field of religion alone, difficulties of entering the mood and vocabulary of a history-making book may lead us to bypass it in favor of easy contemporary ones.

> Augustine, *The City of God; Confessions*
> John Bunyan, *Pilgrim's Progress*
> Dante, *The Divine Comedy*
> *The Little Flowers of St. Francis*
> *The Imitation of Christ*
> John Milton, *Paradise Lost*

Each of these works has passed through hundreds of editions. They stand far below the Bible, but like it deserve to be read eagerly and not simply quoted at second hand. Scores of less distinguished volumes have stood the test of generations; time spent with a work sifted by at least a generation or two is calculated to yield higher returns than time devoted to popular but still untested books.

5. *Stress impact rather than quantity.*

Largely as a result of popular interpretations by a few noted persons, many readers today put great stress upon the rate at

144

which pages are turned. There is an undefined but general impression that significance of your reading hours depends on how many hundred words per minute you succeed in skimming.

So obvious a fallacy hardly needs to be challenged. If you are reading for enlightenment, it makes no difference how many pounds of books you handle each week. One thin volume, slowly pondered, may be more provocative than a shelf of books read at furious pace.

No single speed or manner of reading is suitable for all situations. When searching for facts or following the plot of a novel, it may be desirable to maintain maximum speed. Understanding is far more important than pages per hour in the case of a volume of philosophy or theology. And when brooding over the message of Job or Luke, the question of rate of reading becomes irrelevant.

15

Praise Ye
the Lord!

THIS EXHORTATION IS THE LAST WORD!

Not only is it the closing phrase of the Psalter; it summarizes the mood of that sublime devotional anthology.

Surely it is no accident that the psalms begin with a promise of blessedness to those who ardently seek wisdom day and night —and whose search repeatedly rises to joyous praise. To live continually in such a mood is beyond human capacity; to enter it occasionally is to transform the quality of life. To dwell in it for more frequent and lengthy intervals is to feast on first fruits of the kingdom.

Praise is catalytic, transforming all our values and goals. For praise is directed outward and upward. It is a key that unlocks the prison of the ego. It emphasizes the gulf between Creator and creature. At the same time it remakes the creature into a more vital image of the Creator whom he praises.

To praise, you must be involved. It is not enough to be a passive spectator. There must be uprushing and outgoing. To praise is really to move up and out to meet God, to come into encounter with the divine through that self-emptying which is a fruit of concentration on God's glories.

146

Special Dangers

In some phases of his striving for encounters that evoke praise, a man of the cloth is in a special category. Along the path lurk lions and dragons that ignore all who lack the mark of ordination. These beasts have cultivated such taste that they feed exclusively on flesh of ministers.

1. *Professionalism* is among the most fearful of the monsters that prowl in search of clerical prey.

More than other men, the minister recognizes the significance of public worship and the abiding values of processes that foster the devotional life. But the exercise of his duties requires that he constantly occupy the role of leader.

It is easy to become so absorbed in revealing to others those glories he has found that the leader becomes blind to new wonders. Most professional guides acquire an indefinable but characteristic "mechanical quality" in speech and manner. Having conducted half a hundred tours through a cavern, describing its outstanding features in similar terms each time, a guide has little vitality. His message has no more dynamic than a tape-recorded sales appeal booming through a variety store.

Complexity and extent of the terrain in which he functions give the minister more opportunity for variety than is afforded the typical guide. Still, his absorption with showing others tends to inhibit his own vital participation in such creative exercises as public worship.

Our everyday vocabulary includes buried allusions to the ease with which religious leadership degenerates into putting on a performance. "Patter," the usual label for glib but empty speech of a showman, was formed as a jibe at the way some medieval priests hurried through a toneless Pater Noster. Whether in

Latin or English, the repetition of the Lord's Prayer can be mechanical.

No matter what the nature of his activities, one who is mocked as "going through the motions" perpetuates recognition that a leader may make all the prescribed motions of religious ritual without himself being involved in the ceremony. Much lifeless mumbling of a sublime phrase caused it to be telescoped and added to the jargon of the sideshow; "This is the body of the Son," *Hoc est corpus filii*, degenerated into hocus-pocus.

Part of Kierkegaard's bitter *Attack Upon Christendom* comes to focus here. No heresy or sin, he insists, is so abhorrent to God as surrender to the role of the official. Official words are like those from a handbook or a music box; they evoke no response at all—not even a bad taste in the mouth. "No, the disgusting thing about the official is that one finds it so insipid because it tastes of nothing at all, because one gets no more taste from it than (to use an old Danish expression) by putting the tongue out of the window to see what the weather is like." [1]

Recognition of the danger is a step toward meeting it.

2. *Activism* tempts us to measure our effectiveness by the amount of activity in which we engage. One who is caught in the clutches of this dreadful beast may be more concerned with the number of persons who hear him preach than with perpetual rediscovery of the fear of God as a prelude to occupying the pulpit. He is likely to assess the quality of his ministry by the degree of fatigue that grips him after he has made his last call and dismissed the final committee of the evening.

That this is no new temptation is witnessed by the warning: "It is vain for you to rise up early, to sit up late" (Ps. 127:2). Within the church as well as out of it, the organization man is probably as old as man's organizations. In days of cloak and toga, there were counterparts of the man in the gray flannel clericals.

Still, pressures of the institutional system are probably more acute today than in some epochs. It is a commonplace that quotas, drives, goals, and programs developed outside the local congregation demand more and more of our time.

If you surrender to the pressure to measure your ministry by materialistic success standards, the effects on your role as a witness will be profound. Increasingly, you will reduce the time and energy devoted to striving to know God in such fashion that praise is spontaneous. Increasingly, you will minimize the intellectual and spiritual harrowing, planting, and cultivating that are prerequisite to rich harvests of preaching material.

Have you ever poured a carbonated beverage into a glass of ice when the soda was still warm in the bottle? Such an outpouring produces results very quickly; the glass fills almost at once. But a second look reveals that half the glass holds nothing but a thick head—all bubbles, with no substance.

Just so with the sermon poured out without searching, discovering, praising, and painfully shaping for sharing. This warm stuff fills half an hour on Sunday morning, but is all froth and bubbles, with little capacity to quench thirst of listeners. It is not significant to work so hard for tangibles that one is too weary to respond creatively to clues about kingdom goals.

On the 150th anniversary of Lincoln's birth, Carl Sandburg gave a memorial address in the halls of Congress. During most of the hour, movie and television cameras concentrated on the white-haired poet who was prodigal with polished phrases delivered in melodic fashion.

Once, however, the cameras left Sandburg in order to focus

upon the gallery and reveal a youngish woman in short-sleeved dress and thick glasses, sleeping heavily.

Probably she worked hard, labored to get to the Capitol, exerted great energy in order to be inside the chamber at the history-making hour. She worked so long and hard, it may be assumed, that she not only slept through the address—but was immortalized on film in doing so!

Every seeker faces the dilemma of deciding what activities he will pursue, regardless of those things he must neglect. Even the great Apollos, colleague and fellow worker with Paul, had schedule problems and had to defer a visit to Corinth until a "convenient time" (I Cor. 16:12).

Do not fret that conditions of serving God and man offer more opportunities than you or any other man can accept. Take as many as possible and fulfill them as well as you can. Resist with all your power the insistent temptations and pervasive pressures to put secondary things first. Remember that in the only judgment that matters, you will be measured not so much by what you have done as by what you have become.

Every potential leader of the sheep is challenged to use various methods to persuade a flock to follow. He must settle for himself the question of where he will put his primary emphasis. He will be under pressure to focus on parish administration, upon building up an institution, upon striving for many other goals by which fellow men judge our degree of success.

The leader of the sheep who does not concentrate on entering by the door that is the Word made flesh—upon more deeply and fully coming into personal encounter with God's self-revelation—becomes a thief and a robber. He may attract the biggest congregation in the state. He may erect the most costly edifice in his connection. He may be in international demand as a speaker and writer. But he is a thief and a robber if he permits activities of his career to swindle him of time and energy required for continually coming into larger knowledge and fellowship with the Father.

Avenues That Lead to Praise

If you face special dangers because you are a minister, you also have unusual opportunities. When you succeed in achieving creative praise, you have at one stroke fostered not only your own pilgrimage but also your capacity to guide other seekers.

So regarded, praise that brings enlargement is the most fruitful kind of work.

Fervent praise has dynamic impact on the life—and therefore on the public witness—of him who praises. One who gives much of his daily energy to seeking evidences of God has no time to fret. He can see material prizes pass without a twinge of regret, for he is continually in the act of accepting that most glorious of all rewards: a larger understanding of his Creator. Nothing can drive the merry song from the lips of such a man. He is literally the unconquerable.

And the queer thing about it is that our religious vocation leads men to pay us for doing the very things we most eagerly desire to do! Because our congregation or connection provides us with a living, more than any other persons in society ministers are free to devote time and energy to pursuing avenues that lead to praise.

1. *Public worship offers opportunities.*

So long as our eyes are not blinded by the scales of familiarity or excessive concern to guide others in their worship, we can be renewed each time we spend an hour in the sanctuary. Potent and awesome, the holy place of the Most High fosters that pattern of moods which is preliminary to encounter.

At least at intervals you can find the opportunity to sit in a service of worship as a member of the flock rather than as its shepherd. Perhaps it may be necessary to visit services of a different communion in order to escape the spotlight; if so, the effort required will be richly rewarded.

Special days and occasions, from Easter Sunday to a graveside service in a bleak country cemetery, are potentially enriching. Even a slight deviation from routine provides a charged atmosphere in which he who listens will hear the voice of the Lord.

One minister recalls that the most powerful worship experience of his life came when he addressed a congregation of less than fifty. After an early morning flurry of snow, he arrived at the chapel to meet those who had gathered for a Thanksgiving Day service.

Every element in the situation was charged with meaning, for every person occupying a pew was an expectant mother—unwed. Most of them were young; a few not past fifteen. All wore cotton dresses and white sox; all wore wedding bands—plain gold ones for the most part. Some of these girls from the Florence Crittenden Home were in the early stages of pregnancy, but others were nearing their time.

In the hymns and scripture, everyday words accepted casually in most situations suddenly became emotionally explosive: man, home, baby, father, mistake, sin, purity.

What to do? Interpret the Thanksgiving theme in a folksy way, ignoring the dynamic of the situation and avoiding anything that might evoke consciousness of it? Or attempt in love to face the realities of tragedy and haltingly offer as a solution the redemptive love of a heavenly Father?

The choice of the latter alternative stirred the minister and left him permanently changed, if it touched the heart of no listener.

Every worship occasion is potentially as charged as that in which presence of unwed mothers created heightened sensitivity. But we are usually hardened and complacent, and so ignore the electric atmosphere brought about by the presence of the Maker of the heavens and the earth, the sea, and all that in them is.

Whether occupying a visitor's pew or the pastor's chair, you can cultivate the spirit of eager seeking during that worship which precedes the sermon. Each hymn and prayer is an invitation for you to come into personal meeting with Jehovah.

This morning, though I must stand before these people and call the signals, more than any other worshiper I am in need. Light the fires of my own heart as the acolytes bring the living flame to the altar, O God. Whisper thy forgiveness in some phrase of the anthem. As I kneel or bow, let my body be a visible symbol of the fashion in which I really prostrate myself—not in order that men may see, but because I can do no other when I know myself to be in the presence of the Lord of hosts. Reveal to me something new and stirring about thyself, O God, as my eyes fall upon the symbols of the sanctuary and the faces of thy children who have come hungry for bread thou hast called me to break this hour.

Approaching Elwood, Indiana, late one winter afternoon a traveler found himself driving in the direction of the setting sun. Three blocks ahead on the left, he glimpsed a new sanctuary built of stone. It was not the architecture that caught his eye so much as a sign projecting from the edifice. To say that he was

153

startled is to put it mildly, for never before had he seen a church with a red neon sign proclaiming: "1 HOUR CLEANING."

A closer look revealed that he had been blinded by the sun's glare. Actually the sign was attached to a small frame building that nestled against the west end of the place of worship.

But the fruit of the chance insight is suggestive. Ultimately, it touches on the real function of public worship: one-hour cleaning. It is a major aspect of the church's work to invite men to come into the holy place with all their soils and stains, that they may emerge an hour later radiant in spotless garments.

To the degree that such a quest can motivate us, our role as professionals fades into the background and personal worship becomes vital.

2. *Solitary worship is transforming.*

Private seeking for God is not geared to a time schedule and so may be entered under many different circumstances. That this path toward the throne is not more generally followed is partly due to the incessant din and the innumerable appeals of the community. It is much easier to accept an invitation to speak to a civic club or appear on a panel at the P.T.A. than to lock out the world's noises for even one hour of solitary seeking.

In order to be regarded as a good fellow or to take the course of least resistance, we often let ourselves be bullied into activities we do not enjoy and which we know to involve less than creative use of time. That this is no new situation is indicated by Augustine, who warns against the fourth-century prototype of the jolly civic clubber whose program of activity "merely shrivels the mind and dilates the senses, and must be said, therefore, to produce in the soul nothing else than a tumor or a case of mental rickets." [2]

Even if there were fewer causes and campaigns, rallies and conferences, it would be easy to shirk the rigors of solitary worship in favor of activities that on the surface appear to be more productive, more likely to get results.

Thomas Merton goes so far as to warn that we may adopt patterns of busyness in order to escape demands that confront one who withdraws from men's affairs to come face to face with God. There are persons, he says, who actually fear solitude.

They do everything they can to escape it. What is worse, they try to draw everyone else into activities as ceaseless and as devouring as their own. They are great promoters of useless work. They love to organize meetings and banquets and conferences and lectures. They print circulars, write letters, talk for hours on the telephone in order that they may gather a hundred people together in a large room where they will all fill the air with smoke and make a great deal of noise and roar at one another and clap their hands and stagger home at last patting one another on the back with the assurance that they have all done great things to spread the Kingdom of God.[3]

He who of all men best knew the Father was most conscious of need for communion with him. It is not a sidelight, but a basic aspect of Jesus' life that is emphasized by references to instances when he withdrew "into a desert place apart" (Matt. 14:13).

Solitude is a major either/or force. That person who is altogether social, never consciously solitary (or never aware of it, which has much the same implication) is less than truly individual.

That is one of the most frightful aspects of a culture which provides the continuous anesthesia of mass communication. More than those whose jobs require them to conform to a rigid schedule, we ministers have both the opportunity and the motive to engage in that praise which stems from solitary worship.

Few days—and certainly, few weeks—pass without affording a special opportunity to slip into a house of worship at an hour when it is empty of men. Whether the place be an ornate cathedral or the plainest of rural meeting houses, it fosters the probability of an encounter such as that in which Isaiah saw Jehovah high and lifted up or that in which Francis of Assisi heard the Saviour demand his life as a gift.

He who emerges from such an hour is not the same person who entered. John lent first his ears and then his eyes as God spoke to him through one who had the appearance of the Son of man. "And when I saw him," he said, "I fell at his feet as dead" (Rev. 1:17).

Perhaps there is more than a sublime metaphor involved in the notion of falling down dead at solitary confrontation by a messenger from God. For there is no rising in new life until we have died to the old. Religion's impact must be destructive if it is to be transforming. A mild, middle-of-the-road, anemic version of Christianity may make men who are moral by the standards of the culture in which they live, but it lacks dynamic to transform creatures with feet of clay into prophets of the Most High.

Prayer, meditation, seeking, and searching in hours apart from receptive participation in public worship will make you a more responsive instrument for sounding notes that are plucked by the fingers of God.

3. *Rites and sacred ceremonies feed the soul.*

A sacred ceremony is essentially dramatized worship leading to an encounter with God and consequent joyful praise. Instead of relying on words, the ceremonial act centers upon physical symbols and other nonverbal avenues leading to deep meaning.

As in the case of the other aspects of worship, a ceremonial rite may be more transforming for the leader than any other participant, provided he so magnifies his own sense of eager anticipation that his role does not come between him and the God he serves.

On a Sunday morning in May, I assisted in an observance of the Lord's Supper in a large Southern church. Five ministers were on the platform. Just before the holy feast began, all of us stepped down to the level of the congregation.

There, shadows of the overhead lights were different; the congregation took on a somewhat different appearance when its members were viewed from their own level rather than from above. At this stage of the ceremony, it became clear that one of its functions is periodically to bring the minister down from the elevation of the pulpit to the level of his people.

Before the Supper was served, all ministers turned toward the table with their backs to the congregation. This is one of the few moments in Protestant worship when the minister places something else above the congregation and for an interval deliberately turns his eyes away from his people.

Such an act hits with fresh impact every time we participate in it, for it reminds us that the object of our devotion is not the influential man in the pew, but God above.

When Chrysostom preached on the meaning of the symbolic re-enactment of the divine sacrifice, he consistently avoided "you" in addressing his listeners. Instead, he employed "we" and "us," to stress his conviction that the man who stands at the altar is as much in need of grace as any poor sinner. It is the special mission of the Supper, said Chrysostom, so to challenge its partakers that "while still on earth we may raise to heaven our dragging thoughts." [4]

Throughout his long and arduous life, John Wesley placed great emphasis on spiritual benefits from the sacrament. In spite of continuous travel and a discipline of study that began before daybreak, during forty years he received Communion on an average of three times a week. Ignatius Loyola, for whom the Mass was the chief sacramental avenue to God, framed a personal prayer that he frequently used as he sought the mingled giving and receiving of personal surrender:

> Soul of Christ, sanctify me.
> Body of Christ, save me.
> Blood of Christ, inebriate me.[5]

A holy rite is not performed for its own sake. It is not a terminus, but a road. It is a way of moving into dynamic encounter with the Lord of whom it lispingly witnesses. Part of its power stems from the fact that unlike a purely verbal pattern of worship and searching, a ceremony appeals to all bodily senses simultaneously while serving to focus attention and arouse emotion.

Kneeling at the altar, we gain new perspectives. We see and hear with new eyes and ears; for the moment, we become new persons. Hence when entered with the certainty that it will bring a fresh assurance of God, any emotion-linked ceremony can be revelatory.

4. *Eager expectancy fosters encounter.*

Even when it lacks the powerful supporting factors of formal worship, expectancy is conducive to divine-human encounter.

A Midwestern radio station that takes pride in its news coverage, offers weekly prizes to listeners who submit tips. Each half hour there is a brief summary of the news, but if an important story breaks as a result of a tip, it is relayed without waiting for the formal news period. Announcers frequently intersperse music with a comment such as: "Stay tuned to this station for the very latest information. Next scheduled news at the half hour; next news break at any moment."

The seeker who has a pattern of daily worship keeps his dial on God's station, as it were. As a result he is likely to receive an unexpected message any moment, in a place far removed from formal religious exercises. Such a state of tuned awareness, or receptivity, is quite different from the practice of listening for the voice of Jehovah only in set times and places.

In those congregations where altar candles are used, they burn to symbolize the presence of God. Flames rise upward as the choir sings and as Scripture is read. Candles glow as worshipers contribute of their material means and while the preacher interprets God's law through the sermon. When the hour of worship is over, acolytes move forward and snuff out the candles.

As a symbol indicating that the holy period has ended, such action is valid. But it can be inverted so that men interpret it to mean God's light-giving Spirit will not again be available until Sunday at 10:30.

Chrysostom reminds us that when we seek God, we do not endeavor to find a place, but the Lord of all places. Jeremiah, he points out, was heard when he cried from a place of squalor. Job met God at a dunghill, and Jonah came into vital encounter with him in the belly of a whale. Therefore, urged the golden-voiced preacher: "you, even if you are in the baths, pray; wherever you are, pray; do not seek for a place to pray in: you yourself are a temple." [6]

Whatever the name applied to such an outlook, it is the key to meetings with Jehovah that produce such joyful exhortations as that which urges: "From the rising of the sun unto the going down of the same the Lord's name is to be praised" (Ps. 113:3). That is, praise is to be our dominant occupation. No matter what comes, this must be in the forefront. Compared with it, the importance of making a living, or gaining a reputation, or writing sermons that pack 'em in becomes negligible.

Why make a living, if its demands crush out life?

Let no ambition, no hope, no interest take first place over praise. If necessary, let some aspects of the job slide. Neglect some things, and omit others.

All day, every day, put praise first. In the Scriptures and among men and the signs of nature, seek for evidences of God and the Way, so dynamic that their finding evokes spontaneous praise at unusual hours and places.

Simply to glance at yourself in a mood of awareness is to be bowled over by awe: "I will praise thee; for I am fearfully and wonderfully made" (Ps. 139:14). To pray kneeling with the eyes shut fosters revelation; but it is equally fruitful, upon occasion, to pray with the eyes wide open and no words formed.

Stand erect like a man (no other creature can do it) and hold up your glorious hands in silent dedication to Jehovah and in thanksgiving to him for these unique gifts. See these living tools, ponder their mystery, recall Whitman's line: "the hinge in my hand is more marvelous than all machinery." Firmly resolve to use these hands in ways befitting their marvelous dignity and their grandeur as gifts of the Creator to you—very personal, intimate, and astounding.

Vow with the psalmist, "I will praise thy name for ever and

ever" (Ps. 145:2). Fifty times a day (how high a goal; is it possible?) let encounter with persons and things evoke the Name. "Jehovah. Jehovah did it!"

A barefoot, gold-toothed seller of holly smiles from the street-corner: *Jehovah made her so she could smile.* A traffic light flashes from green to red: *The Lord shaped and sustained those forces that made possible traffic lights and my seeing of them.* A dandelion seed drifts by, transported by its gossamer parachute: *Before the mountains were brought forth, our Creator designed this fragile carrier of precious cargo.*

A pine log glows from the fireplace. It is a mystery hidden through all ages from the beginning of time and now revealed. For fifty years this piece of wood was "tree"—compounded of air, soil, water, and energy from the distant sun. Before it became a tree, it was a seed. Before it was a seed, it was a flower. Molecules of oxygen that enter into the revealing of the mystery of fire were among the primary constituents of this planet, pursuing in obedience to our Creator their many-sided destiny until this very hour.

Whatever the occasion, regardless of the circumstances, God can stir you into such invigorating discovery that true worship takes place, culminating in praise that brings joy into your heart and testimony to your lips. To the degree that you succeed in so listening and hearing, at one stroke you overcome all the problems of finding material for your work as a public witness. Simultaneously, without effort, you appropriate the abundant life more fully than ever before.

NOTES

Chapter 1

1. Eliot Dale Hutchinson, *How to Think Creatively* (Nashville: Abingdon Press, 1949).
2. Jacques Maritain, *Creative Intuition in Art and Poetry* (New York: Pantheon Books, 1953).
3. Jacques Maritain, *Art and Scholasticism* (New York: Charles Scribner's Sons, 1942), p. 23.

Chapter 2

1. Alfred North Whitehead, *The Aims of Education* (New York: The Macmillan Company, 1929), p. 147.
2. William Ernest Hocking, *The Meaning of God in Human Experience* (New Haven: Yale University Press, 1922), vii.
3. Walter Weir, "How to Get More Creative Advertising," *Printer's Ink*, August 17, 1956.
4. Cited in Gerald Kennedy, *With Singleness of Heart* (New York: Harper & Brothers, 1951), p. 133.

Chapter 3

1. Charles A. Bennett, *A Philosophical Study of Mysticism* (New Haven: Yale University Press, 1923), xii.
2. William Blake, *Selected Prose and Poetry* (New York: Modern Library, 1953), p. 403. Edited by Northrop Frye.
3. Cited in Evelyn Underhill, *Mysticism* (New York: Noonday Press, Meridian Books, 1955), p. 10.

Chapter 5

1. W. Somerset Maugham, *The Summing Up* (New York: The Literary Guild of America, Inc., 1938), p. 62.

Chapter 6

1. Henry David Thoreau, *Walden*, ch. 12.

Chapter 7

1. Augustine, *Confessions* (New York: Fathers of the Church, Inc., 1953), XXI, 330.
2. Gilbert K. Chesterton, *The Everlasting Man* (New York: Dodd, Mead & Company, 1925), p. 256.
3. Bernard, *The Steps of Humility* (Cambridge, Mass.: Harvard University Press, 1940), p. 45.

Chapter 9

1. *Letters of Samuel Taylor Coleridge*, "Letter to Poole," March 23, 1801.
2. *Picasso, Forty Years of His Art*. (By permission of the Museum of Modern Art, publishers.)
3. John Bunyan, *Pilgrim's Progress*.
4. *Meister Eckhart*, tr. Raymond B. Blakney (New York: Harper & Brothers, Torchbook, 1957), pp. 10 ff.
5. Evelyn Underhill, op. cit., p. 22.
6. Walt Whitman, *Leaves of Grass*, "Song of Myself" (New York: Doubleday, Doran & Co., Inc. 1940), pp. 67, 99.
7. George Santayana, *Dialogues in Limbo* (Ann Arbor: University of Michigan Press, 1957), p. 14.
8. Cited in M. F. Toal, tr., *Sunday Sermons of the Great Fathers* (Chicago: Henry Regnery Co., 1958), II, 393.
9. Cited in Henry Seidel Canby, *Thoreau* (Boston: Houghton Mifflin Co., 1939), p. 401.
10. Cited in M. F. Toal, op. cit., I, 117.

Chapter 10

1. Miguel de Unamuno, *Tragic Sense of Life* (New York: Dover Publications, 1954), xix.
2. *Sammtliche Werke*, Pt. II, Vol. IV, p. 25.

Chapter 11

1. Charles Dickens, *Pickwick Papers*, ch. 16.
2. Cited in E. S. Bogardus, *Leaders and Leadership* (New York: Appleton-Century, 1934), p. 85.
3. Cited in George M. Stratton, *Anger: Its Religious and Moral Significance* (New York: The Macmillan Company, 1923), p. 62.
4. Cited in Evelyn Underhill, *op. cit.*, p. 222.
5. Miguel de Unamuno, *op. cit.*, p. 330.

Chapter 12

1. Johan Huizinga, *Waning of the Middle Ages* (London: E. Arnold & Co., 1927), p. 173.
2. Albert Schweitzer, *Out of My Life and Thought* (New York: Henry Holt & Co., 1933), p. 185.
3. Alfred North Whitehead, *The Aims of Education*, pp. 50 ff.
4. Herbert Read, *op. cit.*, p. 141.
5. Augustine, *op. cit.*, XXI, 276.
6. Ortega y Gasset, *The Dehumanization of Art* (New York: Doubleday & Co., Anchor Books, 1956), p. 157.
7. Karl Jaspers, essay in *Existentialism*, ed. Walter Kaufman (New York: Meridian Books, 1957), p. 184.
8. *Albert Schweitzer, An Anthropology*, ed. Charles R. Joy (New York: Harper & Brothers), p. 79.

Chapter 13

1. Cited in Max Schoen, *Art and Beauty* (New York: The Macmillan Company, 1932), pp. 60 ff.
2. Collier's report on Coleridge's Eighth Lecture. Cited in R. D. Havens, *The Mind of a Poet* (Baltimore: Johns Hopkins Press, 1941), p. 483.

3. Walt Whitman, op. cit., p. 76.
4. Henry David Thoreau, op. cit., ch. 5.
5. Bernard Berenson, *Aesthetics and History* (London: Constable Publishers, 1954), p. 68.
6. Miguel de Unamuno, op. cit., p. 141.
7. Thomas Merton, *The Sign of Jonas* (New York: Harcourt, Brace & Co., 1953), p. 280.

Chapter 14

1. Alfred North Whitehead, *Dialogues of Alfred North Whitehead,* ed. by Lucien Price (Boston: Little, Brown & Co., 1954), p. 8.
2. Hugh of St. Cher, cited in C. W. Dugmore ed., *The Interpretation of the Bible* (London: Society for Promoting Christian Knowledge, 1944), p. 34.
3. Leo Stein, *Appreciation: Painting, Poetry and Prose* (New York: Random House, Modern Library), p. 170.
4. Herbert Read, op. cit.
5. From *Murder in the Cathedral* by T. S. Eliot. Copyright, 1935, by Harcourt, Brace and Company, Inc., and reprinted with their permission for U. S. distribution. Permission for Canadian rights by Faber and Faber.

Chapter 15

1. Sören Kierkegaard, *Attack upon Christendom,* tr. Walter Lowrie (Boston: Beacon Press, 1956), p. 153.
2. Augustine, *Magnitude of the Soul,* tr. John J. McMahon (New York: Cima Publishing Co., Inc., 1947), II, 96.
3. Thomas Merton, *Seeds of Contemplation* (New York: Dell Books, 1949), p. 53. Copyright, Our Lady of Gethsemane Monastery; used by permission.
4. M. F. Toal, tr., op. cit., II, 139.
5. Ignatius Loyola, *Spiritual Exercises* (New York: Catholic Book Publishing Co., 1948), p. 20.
6. M. F. Toal, trans. op. cit., II, 395.

INDEX TO SCRIPTURE PASSAGES

INDEX OF NAMES AND SUBJECTS

    172

174